AAT

Management Accounting: Costing

Level 3

Advanced Diploma in
Accounting

Question Bank

For assessments from
September 2017

Second edition 2017

ISBN 9781 5097 1259 5

British Library Cataloguing-in-Publication Data
A catalogue record for this book is available from the British Library

Published by

BPP Learning Media Ltd
BPP House, Aldine Place
142-144 Uxbridge Road
London W12 8AA

www.bpp.com/learningmedia

Printed in the United Kingdom

We are grateful to the AAT for permission to reproduce the sample assessment(s). The answers to the sample assessment(s) have been published by the AAT. All other answers have been prepared by BPP Learning Media Ltd.

Contents

		Page
Introduction		iv

Question and answer bank

Chapter tasks		**Questions**	**Answers**
Chapter 1	Introduction to management accounting	3	95
Chapter 2	Cost classification and cost behaviour	7	98
Chapter 3	Materials costs and inventory valuation	15	102
Chapter 4	Labour costs	23	109
Chapter 5	Allocation and apportionment	34	115
Chapter 6	Absorption costing	43	119
Chapter 7	Job, batch and service costing	47	122
Chapter 8	Process costing – losses	52	126
Chapter 9	Process costing – WIP	55	129
Chapter 10	Budgeting: fixed and flexed budgets	62	134
Chapter 11	Variance analysis	67	139
Chapter 12	Cost bookkeeping	73	143
Chapter 13	Marginal costing	77	145
Chapter 14	Short-term decision making	80	148
Chapter 15	Long-term decision making	86	153
AAT AQ2016 sample assessment 1		161	177
AAT AQ2016 sample assessment 2		187	
BPP practice assessment 1		191	207
BPP practice assessment 2		219	235
BPP practice assessment 3		247	263

Introduction

This is BPP Learning Media's AAT Question Bank for *Management Accounting: Costing*. It is part of a suite of ground-breaking resources produced by BPP Learning Media for AAT assessments.

This Question Bank has been written in conjunction with the BPP Course Book, and has been carefully designed to enable students to practise all of the learning outcomes and assessment criteria for the units that make up *Management Accounting: Costing*. It is fully up to date as at June 2017 and reflects both the AAT's qualification specification and the sample assessment provided by the AAT.

This Question Bank contains these key features:

- Tasks corresponding to each chapter of the Course Book. Some tasks are designed for learning purposes, others are of assessment standard

- AAT's AQ2016 sample assessment 1 and answers for *Management Accounting: Costing* and further BPP practice assessments

The emphasis in all tasks and assessments is on the practical application of the skills acquired.

VAT

You may find tasks throughout this Question Bank that need you to calculate or be aware of a rate of VAT. This is stated at 20% in these examples and questions.

Approaching the assessment

When you sit the assessment it is very important that you follow the on screen instructions. This means you need to carefully read the instructions, both on the introduction screens and during specific tasks.

When you access the assessment you should be presented with an introductory screen with information similar to that shown below (taken from the introductory screen from one of the AAT's AQ2016 sample assessments for *Management Accounting: Costing*).

> We have provided this **sample assessment** to help you familiarise yourself with our e-assessment environment. It is designed to demonstrate as many as possible of the question types that you may find in a live assessment. It is not designed to be used on its own to determine whether you are ready for a live assessment.

Assessment information:

You have **2 hours and 30 minutes** to complete this sample assessment.

This assessment contains **10 tasks** and you should attempt to complete **every** task.
Each task is independent. You will not need to refer to your answers to previous tasks.
Read every task carefully to make sure you understand what is required.

Where the date is relevant, it is given in the task data.
Both minus signs and brackets can be used to indicate negative numbers **unless** task instructions say otherwise.

You must use a full stop to indicate a decimal point. For example, write 100.57 NOT 100,57 or 100 57
You may use a comma to indicate a number in the thousands, but you don't have to. For example 10000 and 10,000 are both acceptable.

The actual instructions will vary depending on the subject you are studying for. It is very important you read the instructions on the introductory screen and apply them in the assessment. You don't want to lose marks when you know the correct answer just because you have not entered it in the right format.

In general, the rules set out in the AAT sample assessments for the subject you are studying for will apply in the real assessment, but you should carefully read the information on this screen again in the real assessment, just to make sure. This screen may also confirm the VAT rate used if applicable.

A full stop is needed to indicate a decimal point. We would recommend using minus signs to indicate negative numbers and leaving out the comma signs to indicate thousands, as this results in a lower number of key strokes and less margin for error when working under time pressure. Having said that, you can use whatever is easiest for you as long as you operate within the rules set out for your particular assessment.

You have to show competence throughout the assessment and you should therefore complete all of the tasks. Don't leave questions unanswered.

In some assessments, written or complex tasks may be human marked. In this case you are given a blank space or table to enter your answer into. You are told in the assessments which tasks these are (note: there may be none if all answers are marked by the computer).

If these involve calculations, it is a good idea to decide in advance how you are going to lay out your answers to such tasks by practising answering them on a word document, and certainly you should try all such tasks in this Question Bank and in the AAT's environment using the sample assessment.

When asked to fill in tables, or gaps, never leave any blank even if you are unsure of the answer. Fill in your best estimate.

Note that for some assessments where there is a lot of scenario information or tables of data provided (eg tax tables), you may need to access these via 'pop-ups'. Instructions will be provided on how you can bring up the necessary data during the assessment.

Finally, take note of any task specific instructions once you are in the assessment. For example you may be asked to enter a date in a certain format or to enter a number to a certain number of decimal places.

Grading

To achieve the qualification and to be awarded a grade, you must pass all the mandatory unit assessments, all optional unit assessments (where applicable) and the synoptic assessment.

The AAT Level 3 Advanced Diploma in Accounting will be awarded a grade. This grade will be based on performance across the qualification. Unit assessments and synoptic assessments are not individually graded. These assessments are given a mark that is used in calculating the overall grade.

How overall grade is determined

You will be awarded an overall qualification grade (Distinction, Merit, and Pass). If you do not achieve the qualification you will not receive a qualification certificate, and the grade will be shown as unclassified.

The marks of each assessment will be converted into a percentage mark and rounded up or down to the nearest whole number. This percentage mark is then weighted according to the weighting of the unit assessment or synoptic assessment within the qualification. The resulting weighted assessment percentages are combined to arrive at a percentage mark for the whole qualification.

Grade definition	Percentage threshold
Distinction	90–100%
Merit	80–89%
Pass	70–79%
Unclassified	0–69% Or failure to pass one or more assessment/s

Re-sits

Some AAT qualifications such as the AAT Advanced Diploma in Accounting have restrictions in place for how many times you are able to re-sit assessments. Please refer to the AAT website for further details.

You should only be entered for an assessment when you are well prepared and you expect to pass the assessment.

AAT qualifications

The material in this book may support the following AAT qualifications: AAT Advanced Diploma in Accounting Level 3, AAT Advanced Diploma in Accounting at SCQF Level 6 and Further Education and Training Certificate: Accounting Technician (Level 4 AATSA).

Supplements

From time to time we may need to publish supplementary materials to one of our titles. This can be for a variety of reasons. From a small change in the AAT unit guidance to new legislation coming into effect between editions.

You should check our supplements page regularly for anything that may affect your learning materials. All supplements are available free of charge on our supplements page on our website at:

www.bpp.com/learning-media/about/students

Improving material and removing errors

There is a constant need to update and enhance our study materials in line with both regulatory changes and new insights into the assessments.

From our team of authors BPP appoints a subject expert to update and improve these materials for each new edition.

Their updated draft is subsequently technically checked by another author and from time to time, non-technically checked by a proof reader.

We are very keen to remove as many numerical errors and narrative typos as we can but given the volume of detailed information being changed in a short space of time we know that a few errors will sometimes get through our net.

We apologise in advance for any inconvenience that an error might cause. We continue to look for new ways to improve these study materials and would welcome your suggestions. If you have any comments about this book, please email nisarahmed@bpp.com or write to Nisar Ahmed, AAT Head of Programme, BPP Learning Media Ltd, BPP House, Aldine Place, London W12 8AA.

Question Bank

Chapter 1 – Introduction to management accounting

Task 1.1

Drag and drop the correct answers into the table below:

Annual
External to the organisation
Historic
Historic and future
Internal management
Specified by law
To be useful
When required

	Financial accounting	Management accounting
Users		
Timing		
Type of information		
Format		

Task 1.2

Drag and drop the correct answers into the table below:

Materials
Non-production overheads
Prime cost
Production cost
Production overheads
Total cost

Cost card	£
Direct [ ]	X
Direct labour	X
Direct expenses	X
[ ]	X
[ ]	X
[ ]	X
[ ]	
– selling and distribution	X
– administration	X
– finance	X
[ ]	X

Task 1.3

For which of the following is a profit centre manager normally responsible?

	✓
Costs only	
Revenues only	
Costs and revenues	
Costs, revenues and investments	

Task 1.4

Prime cost is:

	✓
All costs incurred in manufacturing a product	
The total of direct costs	
The material cost of a product	
The cost of operating a department	

Task 1.5

You are an accounts assistant at J Co, a business which makes wooden toy soldiers. You have been asked to present a cost card for the toy soldiers using the following information.

Drag and drop the correct answers into the table below and insert the corresponding figures:

	£
Advertising and sales promotion	0.70
Hire of special tools	0.50
Rent, rates, light and heat	0.30
Toy makers' wages	3.00
Wood and paint	3.50

Cost card – toy soldier	£
Direct materials	
Direct labour	
Direct expenses	
Prime cost	
Production cost	
Non-production overheads:	
Total cost	

BPP
LEARNING MEDIA

5

Task 1.6

Match the fundamental ethical principle to the correct description below by dragging the appropriate option into the table.

Description	Principle
Complying with relevant laws and regulations	
Not disclosing information to third parties without authority	
Being straightforward and honest in all professional and business relationships	
Not allowing bias or conflict of interest	
Maintaining professional knowledge and skill	

Professional competence and due care

Integrity

Confidentiality

Professional behaviour

Objectivity

Task 1.7

Segmented cost is:

	✓
All revenues relating to a particular product made by the business	
The total of direct costs relating to a particular product made by the business	
The material cost relating to a particular product made by the business	
The costs relating to a component of the business which generates revenue	

Chapter 2 – Cost classification and cost behaviour

Task 2.1

Drag and drop the correct entries into the table below, based on whether each one would be classified as a production cost, a selling and distribution cost or an administration cost:

Depreciation of delivery vans
Depreciation of plant and machinery
Factory heat and light
Finance Director's salary
Fuel and oil for delivery vans
Sales Director's salary

Cost types	
Production cost	
Selling and distribution cost	
Administration cost	

Task 2.2

Which of the following would be classed as indirect labour?

	✓
A coach driver in a transport company	
Machine operators in a milk bottling plant	
A maintenance assistant in a factory maintenance department	
Plumbers in a construction company	

Task 2.3

Which of the following items would be treated as an indirect cost?

	✓
Wood used to make a chair	
Metal used for the legs of a chair	
Fabric to cover the seat of a chair	
Staples to fix the fabric to the seat of a chair	

Task 2.4

A company employs three drivers to deliver goods to its customers. The salaries paid to these drivers are:

	✓
A part of prime cost	
A direct production expense	
A production overhead	
A selling and distribution overhead	

Task 2.5

L Ltd is a badminton racquet manufacturer.

Drag and drop the correct entries into the box below to match the correct cost type to each cost item.

Administration costs
Direct labour
Direct materials
Indirect labour
Selling and distribution costs

Cost types	
Carbon for racquet heads	
Office stationery	
Wages of employees stringing racquets	
Supervisors' salaries	
Advertising stand at badminton tournaments	

Task 2.6

Look at the two graphs below. **What costs do they depict?**

Graph A

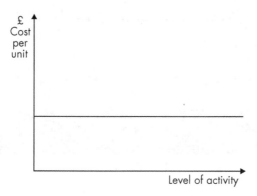

Graph B

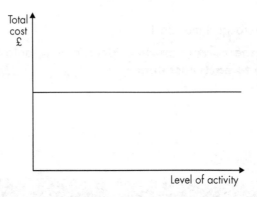

Level of activity

Graph A

	✓
Variable cost per unit	
Fixed cost per unit	
Total fixed cost across level of activity	
Total variable cost	

Graph B

	✓
Variable cost per unit	
Fixed cost per unit	
Total fixed cost across level of activity	
Total variable cost	

Task 2.7

Calculate the fixed and variable elements of the following costs using the high-low technique:

Month	Output Units	Total cost £
January	16,000	252,500
February	18,500	290,000
March	24,000	372,500
April	26,500	410,000
May	25,500	395,000

The following information relates to Tasks 2.8 to 2.12

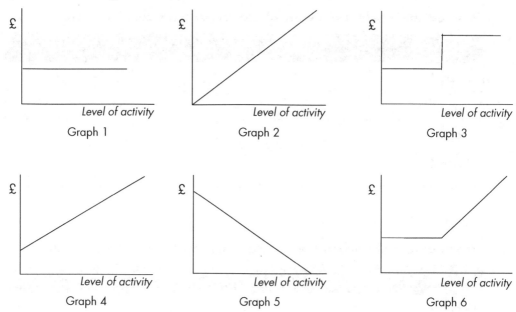

Graph 1

Graph 2

Graph 3

Graph 4

Graph 5

Graph 6

Which one of the above graphs illustrates the costs described in tasks 2.8 to 2.12?

Task 2.8

A variable cost – when the vertical axis represents cost incurred.

	✓
Graph 1	
Graph 2	
Graph 4	
Graph 5	

Task 2.9

A fixed cost – when the vertical axis represents cost incurred.

	✓
Graph 1	
Graph 2	
Graph 3	
Graph 6	

Task 2.10

A variable cost – when the vertical axis represents cost per unit.

	✓
Graph 1	
Graph 2	
Graph 3	
Graph 6	

Task 2.11

A semi-variable cost – when the vertical axis represents cost incurred.

	✓
Graph 1	
Graph 2	
Graph 4	
Graph 5	

Task 2.12

A step fixed cost – when the vertical axis represents cost incurred.

	✓
Graph 3	
Graph 4	
Graph 5	
Graph 6	

Task 2.13

A company has recorded the following data in the two most recent periods.

Total costs of production £	Volume of production Units
13,500	700
18,300	1,100

What is the best estimate of the company's fixed costs per period?

	✓
£13,500	
£13,200	
£5,100	
£4,800	

Task 2.14

We usually classify short-term costs into fixed, variable, step-fixed or semi-variable but in the long run, all costs are:

	✓
Fixed	
Variable	
Step-fixed	
Semi-variable	

Task 2.15

The following information is available for product Zed for the month of January.

Production costs:

Variable   £8 per unit

Fixed   £12,000

What is the total production cost of producing 8,000 units of product Zed in January?

£	

Chapter 3 – Materials costs and inventory valuation

Task 3.1

Paris Ltd manufactures a product the Lipsy, which requires plastic handles PH5:

- Annual demand 90,000 kilograms
- Annual holding cost per kilogram £1
- Fixed ordering cost £2

(a) **Calculate the Economic Order Quantity (EOQ) for PH5.**

The inventory record shown below for plastic grade PH5 for the month of September has only been fully completed for the first three weeks of the month.

(b) **Complete the entries in the inventory record for the two receipts on 24 and 28 September that were ordered using the EOQ method (giving total cost to the nearest whole number).**

(c) **Complete ALL entries in the inventory record for the two issues in the month and for the closing balance at the end of September using the FIFO method of issuing inventory. (Show the costs per kilogram (kg) in £s to 3 decimal places; and the total costs in whole £s.)**

Inventory record for plastic grade PH5:

Date	Receipts Quantity kg	Cost per kg £	Total cost £	Issues Quantity kg	Cost per kg £	Total cost £	Balance Quantity kg	Total cost £
Balance as at 22 September							150	180
24 September		1.398						
26 September				400				
28 September		1.402						
30 September				500				

Task 3.2

Calculate the closing inventory value at 31 March using FIFO by completing the entries in the inventory record below. Enter the cost per unit to 1 decimal place and the total cost to the nearest whole pound.

Inventory record

Date	Receipts			Issues			Balance	
	Quantity kg	Cost per kg £	Total cost £	Quantity kg	Cost per kg £	Total cost £	Quantity kg	Total cost £
Balance as at 1 January							4,000	10,000
31 January	1,000		2,000					
15 February				3,000		7,500		
28 February	1,500		3,750					
14 March				500		1,250		

Task 3.3

Using the AVCO method calculate the cost of materials issues and the value of closing inventory using the information below.

Enter your answer onto the inventory record below. Important! Enter the cost per kg to 2 decimal places. Enter the total cost to the nearest whole pound.

1 January	Balance	300 kg	£25 per unit
2 January	Issue	250 kg	
12 January	Receipt	400 kg	£25.75 per unit
21 January	Issue	200 kg	
29 January	Issue	75 kg	

Inventory Record Card

	Purchases			Requisitions			Balance	
			Total			Total		Total
Date	Quantity	Cost	cost	Quantity	Cost	cost	Quantity	cost
	kg	£	£	kg	£	£	kg	£
1 Jan								
2 Jan								
12 Jan								
21 Jan								
29 Jan								

Task 3.4

Fill in the table below using FIFO to calculate the closing valuation at 31 March.

Inventory record

Date	Receipts Quantity kg	Cost per kg £	Total cost £	Issues Quantity kg	Cost per kg £	Total cost £	Balance Quantity kg	Total cost £
1 January	4,000	2.50	10,000				4,000	10,000
31 January	1,000		2,000					
15 February				3,000				
28 February	1,500	2.50					3,500	8,250
14 March				500				

Task 3.5

Fill in the table below using LIFO to calculate the closing valuation at 31 March.

Inventory record

| Date | Receipts | | | Issues | | | Balance | |
	Quantity kg	Cost per kg £	Total cost £	Quantity kg	Cost per kg £	Total cost £	Quantity kg	Total cost £
1 January	4,000	2.50	10,000				4,000	10,000
31 January	1,000	2.00						
15 February				3,000				
28 February	1,500	2.50						
14 March				500				

Task 3.6

Sheap Ltd had the following containers of juice in inventory:

Date purchased	Quantity	Cost per container £	Total cost £
April 28	840	19.0	15,960
May 4	960	24.5	23,520
May 10	480	28.9	13,872

Drag and drop the correct cost into the cost column of the table on the next page to record issuing 850 of these containers on 11 May and to record the inventory balance after the issue using:

- AVCO (weighted average cost)
- FIFO (first in, first out)
- LIFO (last in, first out)

	Cost £
AVCO issue	
FIFO issue	
LIFO issue	
AVCO balance	
FIFO balance	
LIFO balance	

£33,462	£37,147
£16,205	£22,937
£23,275	£14,455
£30,415	£19,890

Task 3.7

A company wishes to minimise its inventory costs. Order costs are £10 per order and holding costs are £0.10 per unit per month. Fall Co estimates **annual** demand to be 5,400 units.

The economic order quantity is ⬚ **units.**

Task 3.8

The following data relates to component L512:

Ordering costs	£100 per order
Inventory holding costs	£8 per unit per annum
Annual demand	1,225 units

The economic order quantity is ⬚ **units (to the nearest whole unit).**

Task 3.9

The following data relate to inventory item A452:

Average usage   100 units per day

Minimum usage   60 units per day

Maximum usage   130 units per day

Lead time   20–26 days

EOQ   4,000 units

The maximum inventory level was ⬚ **units.**

Task 3.10

Identify whether the following statements are true or false.

Statement	True ✓	False ✓
Issues of inventory using first in, first out (FIFO) will always be costed at the latest purchase price.		
Just-in-time (JIT) involves keeping inventory levels to a minimum.		
Just-in-time (JIT) depends on having reliable suppliers.		

Chapter 4 – Labour costs

Task 4.1

Below is a weekly timesheet for one of Paris Ltd's employees, who is paid as follows:

- For a basic seven-hour shift every day from Monday to Friday – basic pay

- For any overtime in excess of the basic seven hours, on any day from Monday to Friday – the extra hours are paid at time-and-a-third (basic pay plus an overtime premium equal to a third of basic pay)

- For three contracted hours each Saturday morning – basic pay

- For any hours in excess of three hours on Saturday – the extra hours are paid at double time (basic pay plus an overtime premium equal to basic pay)

- For any hours worked on Sunday – paid at double time (basic pay plus an overtime premium equal to basic pay)

Complete the columns headed Basic pay, Overtime premium and Total pay:

(Notes: Zero figures should be entered in cells where appropriate; Overtime pay is the premium amount paid for the extra hours worked).

Employee's weekly timesheet for week ending 14 May

Employee: H. Hector			Cost Centre: Lipsy calibration			
Employee number: LP100			Basic pay per hour: £9.00			

	Hours spent on production	Hours worked on indirect work	Notes	Basic pay £	Overtime premium £	Total pay £
Monday	6	1	10am–11am setting up of machinery			
Tuesday	3	4	9am–1pm department meeting			
Wednesday	8					
Thursday	8					
Friday	6	1	3pm–4pm health and safety training			
Saturday	4					
Sunday	4					
Total	**39**	**6**				

Task 4.2

Paris Ltd is reviewing its overtime payments for employees and has decided to increase basic pay from £9/hr to £10/hr and reduce its payment of overtime as follows. All other terms remain the same.

- For any overtime in excess of the basic seven hours, on any day from Monday to Friday – the extra hours are paid at time-and-a-quarter (basic pay plus an overtime premium equal to a quarter of basic pay)

- For four contracted hours each Saturday morning – basic pay

- For any hours worked on Sunday – paid at time and a half (basic pay plus an overtime premium equal to half of basic pay)

Recalculate the timesheet for H. Hector for the week ending 14 May, taking these changes into account.

Employee: H. Hector			**Cost Centre:** Lipsy calibration			
Employee number: LP100			**Basic pay per hour:** £10.00			

	Hours spent on production	Hours worked on indirect work	Notes	Basic pay £	Overtime premium £	Total pay £
Monday	6	1	10am–11am setting up of machinery			
Tuesday	3	4	9am–1pm department meeting			
Wednesday	8					
Thursday	8					
Friday	6	1	3pm–4pm health and safety training			
Saturday	4					
Sunday	4					
Total	**39**	**6**				

Task 4.3

Paris Ltd has drawn up its payroll records for the month of May. The records show the following details of pay:

	£
Net pay	250,000
PAYE and NIC deductions	62,500
Contributions to company welfare scheme	37,500
Gross pay	350,000

The payroll analysis shows that £275,000 relates to direct labour, and £75,000 is for indirect labour. **The Financial Controller has asked you to record the entries in the ledger in the Wages control account.** Remember Paris Ltd is a manufacturing company, so you need to think about work in progress too. Use the dropdown boxes to enter the line items and enter the relevant figures.

Wages control account

	£			£
Picklist 1 ▼		Picklist 4 ▼		
Picklist 2 ▼		Picklist 5 ▼		
Picklist 3 ▼				

Picklist 1

Bank
Production overhead control
WIP

Picklist 2

HM Revenue and Customs
WIP

Picklist 3

Production overhead control
Welfare scheme contributions

Picklist 4

Bank
HM Revenue and Customs
WIP

Task 4.4

The ledger clerk has forgotten to complete the other entries needed for wages in the work in progress control account and the production overhead control account. **Input the correct entries in the two control accounts below.** Remember that £275,000 relates to direct labour and £75,000 to indirect labour.

Work in progress control account

		£			£
31 May	Wages control				

Production overhead control

		£			£
31 May	Wages control				

Task 4.5

Which one of the following groups of workers would be classified as indirect labour?

	✓
Machinists in an organisation manufacturing clothes	
Bricklayers in a house building company	
Maintenance workers in a shoe factory	

Task 4.6

In a typical cost ledger, the double entry for indirect labour cost incurred is:

			✓
DEBIT Wages control	CREDIT	Overhead control	
DEBIT Admin overhead control	CREDIT	Wages control	
DEBIT Overhead control	CREDIT	Wages control	
DEBIT Wages control	CREDIT	Admin overhead control	

Task 4.7

Extracts are given below from Gloworm Ltd's payroll for March.

Manufacturing department A production employees' wages	£18,500
Manufacturing department B production employees' wages	£22,500
Maintenance department employees' wages	£12,700
General admin department employees' salaries	£7,600

Complete the cost journal entries to record the payroll payments for March.

	Code	Dr £	Cr £
Manufacturing department A wages	▼		
Manufacturing department A wages	▼		
Manufacturing department B wages	▼		
Manufacturing department B wages	▼		
Maintenance department wages	▼		
Maintenance department wages	▼		
General admin department salaries	▼		
General admin department salaries	▼		

Picklist:

3400 Operating overheads
2400 Manufacturing department B direct costs
6000 Wages control account
3500 Non-operating overheads
2300 Manufacturing department A direct costs

Task 4.8

In a typical cost ledger, the double entry for direct wages cost incurred is:

				✔
DEBIT	Wages control	CREDIT	Work in progress account	
DEBIT	Work in progress account	CREDIT	Wages control	
DEBIT	Costs of sales account	CREDIT	Work in progress account	
DEBIT	Finished goods account	CREDIT	Work in progress account	

Task 4.9

Below is a table showing the hours worked by one of XYZ Ltd's employees, who is paid as follows:

- For a basic shift every day from Monday to Friday, the basic pay is £15 per hour.

- For any overtime in excess of the basic hours, on any day from Monday to Friday – the extra hours are paid at time-and-a-half (basic pay plus an overtime premium equal to half of basic pay).

- For any hours worked on Saturday or Sunday the hours are paid at double time (basic pay plus an overtime premium equal to basic pay).

(a) Complete the gaps in the table below to calculate the labour cost (to 2 decimal places).

Employee's weekly timesheet for week ending 7 December

	Hours	Total pay £
Basic pay (including basic hours for overtime)	48	
Mon–Fri overtime premium	7	
Sat–Sun overtime premium	6	
Total		

(b) Employees are also entitled to a bonus of 30% of basic hourly rate for every unit of production in excess of the monthly target. The target for last month was 450 units and employee A produced 480 units.

What was employee A's bonus payment for the month?

£ [ ]

(c) At the end of the month there was a total closing work in progress of 7,000 units which were 60% complete with regard to labour.

What are the equivalent units of production with regard to labour of the closing work in progress? [ ] units

Task 4.10

ABC Ltd produced 42,000 equivalent units of production in June. The total direct labour cost for June was £13,650.

Calculate the total direct labour cost per equivalent unit of the finished production for June.

Give your answer in £s to three decimal places.

£	

Task 4.11

Hopk Ltd has four employees working in department B. They are paid a basic rate of £22.00 per hour, and any overtime is paid at the following rates:

- Overtime rate 1 – basic pay + 50%
- Overtime rate 2 – double the rate of basic rate

Hopk sets a target for number of units produced each month. A bonus equal to 40% of the basic hourly rate is payable for each unit produced in the month in excess of the target.

The target for April for department B was 2,387.5 units; however, the team actually produced 2,987.5 units.

All team members work the same number of hours.
All overtime and bonuses are included as part of the direct labour cost.

(a) Complete the gaps in the table below to calculate the total labour cost for department.

Labour cost	Hours	£
Basic pay	800	
Overtime rate 1	50	
Overtime rate 2	40	
Total cost before bonus	890	
Bonus payment		
Total cost including bonus		

(b) **Calculate the total labour cost of producing each unit in the month of April.**

The total labour cost of producing each unit in the month of April is:

£ [   ] .

There are four employees in department B.

(c) **Complete the following sentence.**

The basic pay and overtime for each member of department B for April was:

£ [   ]   and the bonus payable to each team member was:

£ [   ] .

Chapter 5 – Allocation and apportionment

Task 5.1

Paris Ltd's budgeted overheads for the next financial year are:

	£	£
Depreciation of plant and equipment		2,010,375
Power for production machinery		1,787,500
Rent and rates		261,268
Light and heat		57,750
Indirect labour costs:		
Maintenance	253,750	
Stores	90,125	
General Administration	600,251	
Total indirect labour cost		944,126

The following information is also available:

Department	Net book value of plant and equipment	Production machinery power usage (KwH)	Floor space (square metres)	Number of employees
Production centres:				
Silicon moulding	3,600,000	1,145,000		15
Silicon extrusion	4,400,000	2,430,000		16
Support cost centres:				
Maintenance			8,000	4
Stores			10,000	5
General Administration			10,000	6
Total	8,000,000	3,575,000	28,000	46

Overheads are allocated or apportioned on the most appropriate basis. The total overheads of the support cost centres are then reapportioned to the two production centres using the direct method.

- 35% of the Maintenance cost centre's time is spent maintaining production machinery in the Silicon moulding production centre, and the remainder in the Silicon extrusion production centre.

- The Stores cost centre makes 40% of its issues to the Silicon moulding production centre, and 60% to the Silicon extrusion production centre.

- General Administration supports the two production centres equally.

- There is no reciprocal servicing between the three support cost centres.

Complete the table showing the apportionment and reapportionment of overheads to the two production centres. Round to the nearest pound.

	Basis of apportionment	Silicon moulding £	Silicon extrusion £	Maintenance £	Stores £	General Admin £	Totals £
Depreciation of plant and equipment	NBV of Plant and equipment						
Power for production machinery	Production machinery power usage (KwH)						
Rent and rates	Floor space						
Light and heat	Floor space						
Indirect labour	Allocated						
Totals							
Reapportion Maintenance							
Reapportion Stores							
Reapportion General Admin							
Total overheads to production centres							

Task 5.2

(a) The financial controller at Paris Ltd is reviewing the basis of allocating the costs of the two production centres, and is considering using the number of employees instead of NBV and power usage. **Recalculate the allocations and apportionments using headcount as a basis for these two cost centres. She has also decided that the silicon moulding cost centre uses far more general admin than the extrusion cost centre, and wants you to recalculate the apportionments using a ratio of 65:35.** Use the dropdown screen to remind you of the data in the task.

Dropdown screen

Paris Ltd's budgeted overheads for the next financial year are:

	£	£
Depreciation of plant and equipment		2,010,375
Power for production machinery		1,787,500
Rent and rates		261,268
Light and heat		57,750
Indirect labour costs:		
Maintenance	253,750	
Stores	90,125	
General Administration	600,251	
Total indirect labour cost		944,126

The following information is also available:

Department	Net book value of plant and equipment	Production machinery power usage (KwH)	Floor space (square metres)	Number of employees
Production centres:				
Silicon moulding	3,600,000	1,145,000		15
Silicon extrusion	4,400,000	2,430,000		16
Support cost centres:				
Maintenance			8,000	4
Stores			10,000	5
General Administration			10,000	6
Total	8,000,000	3,575,000	28,000	46

Overheads are allocated or apportioned on the most appropriate basis. The total overheads of the support cost centres are then reapportioned to the two production centres using the direct method.

- 35% of the Maintenance cost centre's time is spent maintaining production machinery in the Silicon moulding production centre, and the remainder in the Silicon extrusion production centre.

- The Stores cost centre makes 40% of its issues to the Silicon moulding production centre, and 60% to the Silicon extrusion production centre.

- General Administration supports the two production centres, with 65% of its costs attributable to Silicon moulding and 35% attributable to Silicon extrusion.

- There is no reciprocal servicing between the three support cost centres.

Complete the table showing the apportionment and reapportionment of overheads to the two production centres.

	Basis of apportionment	Silicon moulding £	Silicon extrusion £	Maintenance £	Stores £	General Admin £	Totals £
Depreciation of plant and equipment	Headcount						
Power for production machinery	Headcount						
Rent and rates	Floor space						
Light and heat	Floor space						
Indirect labour	Allocated						
Totals							
Reapportion Maintenance							
Reapportion Stores							
Reapportion General Admin							
Total overheads to production centres							

(b) **If you were the manager in charge of the silicon moulding cost centre would you be happy with the revised allocations?**

Task 5.3

Product Em has the following estimated costs per unit.

Product Em	£ per unit
Direct materials	5.50
Direct labour	7.20
Variable overheads	1.50
Fixed manufacturing overheads	2.30
Fixed administration, selling and distribution costs	1.70
Total costs	18.20

What is the full absorption cost of one unit of Em?

£	

Task 5.4

Using the following data reapportion the overheads of Stores and Maintenance and General administration overheads to production departments X and Y using the direct method.

	Production		Service centres		
	X £	Y £	Stores £	Maintenance £	General administration overheads £
Allocated & Apportioned overheads	80,000	50,000	40,000	30,000	8,000
Value of machinery	8,000	7,000			

- 55% of the stores department's time is spent on production department X. The remaining time is spent on production department Y.

- The maintenance costs are to be apportioned between the production departments on the basis of value of machinery.

- General administration overheads are to be apportioned equally between the two production departments.

Direct method

	Production		Service centres		
	X £	Y £	Stores £	Maintenance £	General administration overheads £
Overheads					
Reapportion Stores					
Reapportion Maintenance					
Reapportion general admin overheads					
Total					

Task 5.5

Using the following data reapportion the overheads of Stores and Maintenance to production departments X and Y using the step-down method starting with Stores

	Production		Service centres	
	X £	Y £	Stores £	Canteen £
Allocated & Apportioned overheads	80,000	50,000	40,000	30,000
Number of employees	30	50	5	–

- 50% of the stores department's time is spent on production department X. 30% of stores department's time is spent on production department Y. 20% is spent on maintenance.

- The canteen costs are to be apportioned between the production departments on the basis of number of employees.

Step-down method

	Production		Service centres	
	X £	Y £	Stores £	Maintenance £
Allocated overhead				
Apportion stores				
Apportion maintenance				
Total				

Chapter 6 – Absorption costing

Task 6.1

(a) You have been asked to calculate the actual overhead absorbed based on £20 per hour for labour hours and £55 per hour for machine hours, and the following actual hours for labour and machinery:

	Silicon moulding	Silicon extrusion
Actual direct labour hours	21,222	17,144
Actual machine hours	8,459	6,501
Overhead absorbed – labour hrs		
Overhead absorbed – machine hrs		

(b) The actual overheads were found to be £425,799 for silicon moulding and £354,416 for silicon extrusion. Calculate any differences between the actual overheads at the end of the quarter and the overheads absorbed that you have just calculated.

	Silicon moulding	Silicon extrusion
Actual overheads (£)		
Difference – labour hours		
Difference – machine hours		

Task 6.2

Over-absorbed overheads always occur when:

	✓
Absorbed overheads exceed actual overheads	
Absorbed overheads exceed budgeted overheads	
Actual overheads exceed budgeted overheads	

The following information relates to Tasks 6.3 and 6.4

A company has the following actual and budgeted data for year 4.

	Budget	Actual
Labour hours	8,000 hrs	9,000 hrs
Variable production overhead per unit	£3	£3
Fixed production overheads	£360,000	£432,000
Sales	6,000 units	8,000 units

Overheads are absorbed using a rate per unit, based on budgeted labour hours.

Task 6.3

The fixed production overhead absorbed during year 4 was:

	✓
£384,000	
£405,000	
£432,000	
£459,000	

Task 6.4

Fixed production overhead was:

	✓
Under absorbed by £27,000	
Under absorbed by £72,000	
Under absorbed by £75,000	
Over absorbed by £27,000	

Task 6.5

Choose the correct description for each of the three terms below.

Term	Description	
Activity based costing		▼
Cost driver		▼
Cost pool		▼

Picklist:

Assigning only variable costs to cost units
A factor influencing the level of cost
Equivalent to a cost centre in traditional absorption costing
A cost which cannot be traced directly to a product
A unit of product for which costs can be ascertained
Charging whole cost items direct to a cost unit
Identifying activities which cause costs to charge overheads to products

Task 6.6

Paris Ltd has set its budgets and estimated its budgeted overheads and activity levels as follows:

	Silicon moulding	Silicon extrusion
Budgeted overheads (£)	450,000	352,520
Budgeted direct labour hours	25,350	20,475
Budgeted machine hours	8,750	6,350

(a) **What would be the budgeted overhead absorption rate for each department, if this were set based on their both being heavily automated?**

	✓
Silicon moulding £18/hour, Silicon extrusion £17/hour	
Silicon moulding £51/hour, Silicon extrusion £17/hour	
Silicon moulding £51/hour, Silicon extrusion £56/hour	
Silicon moulding £18/hour, Silicon extrusion £56/hour	

(b) **What would be the budgeted overhead absorption rate for each department, if this were set based on their both being labour intensive?**

	✓
Silicon moulding £51/hour, Silicon extrusion £17/hour	
Silicon moulding £18/hour, Silicon extrusion £17/hour	
Silicon moulding £18/hour, Silicon extrusion £56/hour	
Silicon moulding £51/hour, Silicon extrusion £56/hour	

Task 6.7

The financial controller at Paris Ltd has looked at the overhead absorption rates in the two cost centres, and wants a single rate for labour hours and for machinery across the two centres. She has chosen £20/hr for labour hours and £55/hr for machinery.

Recalculate the budgeted direct labour hours and machine hours based on these rates. Give your answers to the nearest whole number. Refer to the table below from the last task:

	Silicon moulding	Silicon extrusion
Budgeted overheads (£)	450,000	352,520
Budgeted direct labour hours		
Budgeted machine hours		

Chapter 7 – Job, batch and service costing

Task 7.1

Drag and drop the correct entries into the box below to match the correct cost unit to a service:

Full-time student
Meal served
Occupied bed-night
Passenger/kilometre, tonne/kilometre
Patient-day

Service	Cost unit
Road, rail and air transport services	
Hotels	
Education	
Hospitals	
Catering establishments	

Task 7.2

Petra Jones is a builder who has issued a quote for a conservatory. Now the job is completed, she would like you to calculate any variances that have arisen. **State whether each variance is favourable or adverse (unfavourable).** The details are in the table below. Input your answers into the right hand column.

Job number 03456

	Budget £	Actual £	Variance F/A £
Direct materials			
Plasterboard	3,600.00	3,500.00	
Wood and door frames	4,750.00	4,802.00	
Insulation	1,050.00	1,145.00	
Electrical fittings	320.00	300.00	
Windows	2,220.00	2,576.00	
Paint	270.00	250.00	
Direct labour			
Construction	554.00	641.00	
Electrical	224.00	160.00	

	Budget £	Actual £	Variance F/A £
Decorating	165.00	205.00	
Direct expenses			
Hire of specialist lathe	240.00	240.00	
Overheads (based on direct lab hrs)			
84/90 hours @ £15.00	1,260.00	1,350.00	

Task 7.3

(a) Petra Jones has also asked you to highlight any variances above 5% for further investigation. Use the table below to make your calculations. Enter the percentages to one decimal place.

(b) She also wants you to calculate the profit on the job, comparing this with the original quotation made based on 20% of total cost.

(c) Calculate the percentage variance between the original profit and the final profit figure. Give your answer to 1 decimal place.

[＿＿＿＿] %

	Budget £	Actual £	Variance F/A £	%
Direct materials				
Plasterboard	3,600.00	3,500.00	100F	
Wood and door frames	4,750.00	4,802.00	52A	
Insulation	1,050.00	1,145.00	95A	
Electrical fittings	320.00	300.00	20F	
Windows	2,220.00	2,576.00	356A	
Paint	270.00	250.00	20F	
Direct labour				
Construction	554.00	641.00	87A	
Electrical	224.00	160.00	64F	
Decorating	165.00	205.00	40A	
Direct expenses				
Hire of specialist lathe	240.00	240.00	0	
Overheads (based on direct lab hrs)				
84/90 hours @ £15.00	1,260.00	1,350.00	90A	
Total cost	14,653.00			
Profit	2,930.60			
Net price	17,583.60			
VAT at 20%	3,516.72			
Total price	21,100.32			

Task 7.4

Which of the following are characteristics of service costing?

	✓
High levels of indirect costs as a proportion of total cost	
Cost units are often intangible	
Use of composite cost units	
Use of equivalent units	

Task 7.5

Product Tee is made in batches of 32,000 units and the following costs are estimated.

Product Tee	£ per batch
Direct materials	176,000
Direct labour	230,400
Variable overheads	48,000
Fixed manufacturing overheads	73,600
Fixed administration, selling and distribution costs	54,400
Total costs	582,400

(a) **Calculate the total cost of one unit of product Tee.**

£ [   ]

(b) **Calculate the full absorption cost of one unit of product Tee.**

£ [   ]

(c) **Calculate the full absorption cost of one batch of product Tee.**

£ [   ]

Chapter 8 – Process costing – losses

Task 8.1

The teeming and lading department of Paris Ltd uses process costing for some of its products.

The process account for October for one particular process has been partly completed but the following information is also relevant:

Two employees worked on this process during October. Each employee worked 37 hours per week for 4 weeks and was paid £12.50 per hour.

Overheads are absorbed on the basis of £10.50 per labour hour.

Paris Ltd expects a normal loss of 10% during this process, which it then sells for scrap at 60p per kg.

(a) **Complete the process account below for October.**

Description	Kg	Unit cost £	Total cost £	Description	Kg	Unit cost £	Total cost £
Material TL4	700	1.35		Normal loss		0.60	
Material TL3	350	1.50		Output			
Material TL9	400	1.25					
Labour							
Overheads							

(b) **Identify the correct journal entries for an abnormal loss.**

	Debit	Credit
Abnormal loss account		
Process account		

Task 8.2

Paris Ltd has reviewed its labour costs and decided to hire two cheaper employees, paying them £9.50 per hour. However they are less experienced and take longer, so they each work 40 hours per week for four weeks. The normal loss goes up to 20% during the process. Overheads continue to be absorbed at £10.50 per labour hour.

Recalculate the process account to take account of these changes.

Description	Kg	Unit cost £	Total cost £	Description	Kg	Unit cost £	Total cost £
Material TL4	700	1.35		Normal loss		0.60	
Material TL3	350	1.50		Output			
Material TL9	400	1.25					
Labour							
Overheads							

Do you think the decision made by management is a good one?

Task 8.3

Paris Ltd makes a product which goes through several processes. The following information is available for the month of June:

	Kg
Opening WIP	4,500
Input	54,300
Normal loss	400
Transferred to finished goods	60,400

What was the abnormal gain in June?

	✓
2,600 kg	
3,000 kg	
2,000 kg	
2,560 kg	

Task 8.4

A food manufacturing process has a normal wastage of 10% of input. In a period, 3,000 kg of material were input and there was an abnormal loss of 75 kg. No inventories are held at the beginning or end of the process.

The quantity of good production achieved was ⬚ **kg.**

Task 8.5

A company makes a product, which passes through a single process.

Details of the process for the last period are as follows:

Materials   5,000 kg at 50p per kg

Normal losses are 10% of input in the process, and without further processing any losses can be sold as scrap for 20p per kg.

The output for the period was 4,200 kg from the process.

There was no work in progress at the beginning or end of the period.

(a) **The value credited to the process account for the scrap value of the normal loss for the period will be**

£ ⬚ **(to the nearest £).**

(b) **The abnormal loss for the period is** ⬚ **kg.**

Chapter 9 – Process costing – WIP

Task 9.1

What is an equivalent unit?

	✓
A unit of output which is identical to all others manufactured in the same process	
Notional whole units used to represent uncompleted work	
A unit of product in relation to which costs are ascertained	
The amount of work achievable, at standard efficiency levels, in an hour	

Task 9.2

G Ltd has a process called H4. During the month of June the costs of that process were £56,000 and the output was 20,400 completed units and 8,000 units that were 25% completed.

What is the cost per equivalent unit?

Task 9.3

(a) Another of G Ltd's processes is the C4. The costs incurred in this process for the month of June are as follows:

Materials   £21,600

Labour and overheads   £13,350

At the end of the period there were 8,300 units of completed output and 1,000 units of closing work in progress. The work in progress has had 70% of its material input and 60% of the labour and overheads input.

Calculate the cost per equivalent unit for materials and labour/overheads.

	Units	Materials		Labour/overheads	
		Proportion complete	Equivalent units	Proportion complete	Equivalent units
Completed		100%		100%	
Work in progress		70%		60%	
Total equivalent units					
Cost per equivalent unit	=			=	

(b) **Find values for the completed output and the closing work in progress.**

	£
Completed output	
Materials	
Labour/overhead	
Work in progress	
Materials	
Labour/overhead	

Task 9.4

Beeb Ltd has the following costs in a period:

Raw materials 4,100 units	£45,100
Labour	£32,608
Overheads	£16,424

Opening WIP: 100 units with a value of £1,220. It was 100% complete for materials, 60% for labour and 30% for overheads.

The split of the £1,220 is:

Materials	£800
Labour	£360
Overheads	£60
	£1,220

Output from this Process: 4,040 units

Closing WIP: 160 units with a value of £2,912. It was also complete as below:

Raw materials	100%	complete
Labour	60%	complete
Overheads	60%	complete

There were no losses.

Required

Prepare a statement of equivalent units using FIFO.

(a) **FIFO**

Statement of equivalent units

	Actual	Equivalent Units		
	Units	Materials	Labour	Overheads
Opening WIP				
Goods started and finished				
Good output				
Closing WIP				
Equivalent units				

(b) **Prepare a statement of cost per equivalent unit**

	£	£	£
Input costs			
Cost per equivalent unit			

(c) **Value the units**

		£
Value of good output =	Costs b/f in opening WIP =	
	Materials	
	Labour	
	Overheads	
Value of Closing WIP =		

(d)   Prepare the process account

Process

	Units	£		Units	£
Opening WIP			Good output		
Raw Materials					
Labour			Closing WIP		
Overheads					

Task 9.5

Beeb Ltd has the following costs in a period:

Raw materials 4,100 units	£45,100
Labour	£32,608
Overheads	£16,424

Opening WIP: 100 units with a value of £1,220. It was 100% complete for materials, 60% for labour and 30% for overheads.

The split of the £1,220 is:

Materials	£800
Labour	£360
Overheads	£60
	£1,220

Output from this Process: 4,040 units

Closing WIP: 160 units with a value of £2,912. It was also complete as below:

Raw materials	100%	complete
Labour	60%	complete
Overheads	60%	complete

There were no losses.

Required

(a) **Prepare a statement of equivalent units using the weighted average method.**

Statement of equivalent units

	Actual	Equivalent units		
	Units	Materials	Labour	Overheads
Good output				
Closing WIP				
Equivalent units				

(b) **Prepare a statement of cost per equivalent unit**

	£	£	£
Costs b/f			
Input costs			
Cost per equivalent unit = Input costs/Equivalent units (to 2dp)			
		Total =	

(c) **Value the units**

Value of good output (to 0 dp) =
Value of Closing WIP (to 0 dp) =

(d) **Prepare the process account**

Process

	Units	£		Units	£
Opening WIP b/f			Output W1		
Raw Materials			Closing WIP c/d		
Labour					
Overheads			Rounding		(21)

Chapter 10 – Budgeting: fixed and flexed budgets

Task 10.1

Paris Ltd has prepared a forecast for the next quarter for one of its small components, PA01. This component is produced in batches, and the forecast is based on producing and selling 3,000 batches.

One of the customers of Paris Ltd has indicated that it may be significantly increasing its order level for component PA01 for the next quarter, and it appears that activity levels of 3,750 batches and 5,000 batches are feasible.

The semi-variable costs should be calculated using the high-low method. If 7,500 batches are sold the total semi-variable cost will be £18,450, and there is a constant unit variable cost up to this volume.

Complete the table below and calculate the estimated profit per batch of PA01 at the different activity levels.

Batches produced and sold	3,000	3,750	5,000
	£	£	£
Sales revenue	60,000		
Variable costs:			
Direct materials	5,700		
Direct labour	27,000		
Overheads	9,300		
Semi-variable costs:	9,450		
Variable element			
Fixed element			
Total cost	51,450		
Total profit	8,550		
Profit per batch (to 2 decimal places)	2.85		

Task 10.2

The financial controller at Paris Ltd has just informed you of the following cost increases and asked you to recalculate the budget at the three activity levels.

Direct materials £2.00/kg. 1 kg is used in each PA01.

Direct labour £10/hr. It takes 1 hour to make a PA01.

Overheads are now £3.20 per PA01.

Complete the table below and calculate the estimated profit per batch of PA01 at the different activity levels.

Batches produced and sold	3,000	3,750	5,000
	£	£	£
Sales revenue	60,000		
Variable costs:			
Direct materials			
Direct labour			
Overheads			
Semi-variable costs:	9,450		
Variable element			
Fixed element			
Total cost			
Total profit			
Profit per batch (to 2 decimal places)			

Task 10.3

A customer has put in an order for 4,000 batches. Production is stopped where the profit per batch is less than £2. Recommend to management whether Paris Ltd should go ahead with the order. **Fill in the table below:**

Batches produced and sold	3,000 £	4,000 £
Sales revenue	60,000	
Variable costs:		
Direct materials	6,000	
Direct labour	30,000	
Overheads	9,600	
Semi-variable costs:		
Variable element	6,000	
Fixed element	3,450	
Total cost	55,050	
Total profit	4,950	
Profit per batch (to 2 decimal places)	1.65	

Choose the correct option below.

Paris Ltd should accept/reject the order for 4,000 units.

Task 10.4

Claridges Ltd has prepared a forecast for the next quarter for one of its small Metal components, the zigger. This component is produced in batches and the forecast is based on selling and producing 3,000 batches.

One of the customers of Claridges Ltd has indicated that it may be significantly increasing its order level for the zigger for the next quarter, and it appears that activity levels of 5,000 batches and 7,000 batches are feasible.

The semi-variable costs should be calculated using the high-low method. If 7,500 batches are sold the total semi-variable cost will be £18,450, and there is a constant unit variable cost up to this volume.

Complete the table below and calculate the estimated profit per batch of the zigger at the different activity levels:

Batches produced and sold	3,000 £	5,000 £	7,000 £
Sales revenue	90,000		
Variable costs:			
Direct materials	13,500		
Direct labour	31,500		
Overheads	18,000		
Semi-variable costs:	9,450		
Variable element			
Fixed element			
Total cost	72,450		
Total profit	17,550		
Profit per batch (to 2 decimal places)	5.85		

Task 10.5

CCC Ltd has prepared a forecast for the next quarter for one of its products. The products are produced in batches and the forecast is based on selling and producing 4,000 batches.

The managing director would like to expand the business and is interested to know the profits that could be made if 6,000 batches were made and sold and 9,000 batches were made and sold.

The semi-variable costs should be calculated using the high-low method. If 6,500 batches are sold the total semi-variable cost will be £24,250, and there is a constant unit variable cost up to this volume.

Complete the table below and calculate the estimated profit per batch of the product at the different activity levels:

Batches produced and sold	4,000 £	6,000 £	9,000 £
Sales revenue	140,000		
Variable costs:			
Direct materials	22,000		
Direct labour	50,000		
Overheads	28,000		
Semi-variable costs:	16,750		
Total cost	116,750		
Total profit	23,250		
Profit per batch (to 2 decimal places)	5.81		

Chapter 11 – Variance analysis

Task 11.1

Paris Ltd has the following original budget and actual performance for product SHEP for the year ending 30 September:

	Budget	Actual
Volume sold	150,000	156,000
	£000	£000
Sales revenue	1,200	1,326
Less costs:		
Direct materials	375	372
Direct labour	450	444
Overheads	225	250
Operating profit	150	260

Both direct materials and direct labour are variable costs, but the overheads are fixed.

Complete the table below to show a flexed budget and the resulting variances against this budget for the year. Show the actual variance amount for sales, each cost, and operating profit, in the column headed 'Variance' and indicate whether this is Favourable or Adverse by entering F or A in the final column. If neither F nor A enter 0.

	Flexed Budget	Actual	Variance	Favourable F or Adverse A
Volume sold		156,000		
	£000	£000	£000	
Sales revenue		1,326		
Less costs:				
Direct materials		372		
Direct labour		444		
Overheads		250		
Operating profit		260		

Task 11.2

The Managing Director of Paris Ltd has asked you to explain why the actual outcome was better than budgeted. He wants you to do some calculations and suggest reasons why the revenues and costs may be better than budgeted.

Input your calculations to two decimal places into the table below, in the two right hand columns. Ignore overheads.

	Flexed Budget	Actual	Budget unit cost/revenue	Actual unit cost/revenue
Volume sold	156,000	156,000		
	£000	£000		
Sales revenue	1,248	1,326		
Less costs:				
Direct materials	390	372		
Direct labour	468	444		
Overheads	225	250		
Operating profit	165	260		

Are the following true or false?

The unit selling price difference may be due to a rise in the sales price not planned in the budget.	True/False
The unit selling price difference may be due to fewer bulk discounts to customers	True/False
The materials unit price difference may be due to bulk buying discounts.	True/False
The materials unit price difference may be due to a cheaper source of supply.	True/False
The labour cost difference may be due to having more lower paid employees.	True/False
The labour cost difference may be due to efficiency savings.	True/False

Task 11.3

Balloonz Ltd had budgeted to manufacture and sell 40,000 packets of balloons last year. However, due to a shortage of staff, it was only able to manufacture and sell 32,000 packets. Balloonz Ltd's manufacturing costs are all variable except for fixed overheads.

Complete the table below to show a flexed budget and the resulting variances against the budget for the year. Show the actual variance amount for sales revenue and each cost in the column headed 'Variance'.

Note:

- **Adverse variances must be denoted with a minus sign or brackets.**

- **Enter 0 where any figure is zero.**

	Original budget	Flexed budget	Actual	Variance
Number of packets	40,000	32,000	32,000	
	£	£	£	£
Sales revenue	130,000		96,000	
Less costs:				
Direct materials and direct labour	48,000		36,800	
Variable overheads	22,000		19,200	
Fixed overheads	14,200		13,600	
Profit from operations	45,800		26,400	

Task 11.4

Pumpken Ltd had budgeted to manufacture and sell 60,000 books in May. However, due to some bad publicity, it was only able to manufacture and sell 45,000 books. Pumpken's manufacturing costs are all variable except for fixed overheads.

Complete the table below to show a flexed budget and the resulting variances against the budget for May. Show the actual variance amount for sales revenue and each cost in the column headed 'Variance'.

Note:

- **Adverse variances must be denoted with a minus sign or brackets.**

- **Enter 0 where any figure is zero.**

	Original budget	Flexed budget	Actual	Variance
Number of books	60,000	45,000	45,000	
	£	£	£	£
Sales revenue	1,140,000		910,200	
Less costs:				
Direct materials and direct labour	480,000		375,000	
Variable overheads	540,000		406,400	
Fixed overheads	56,000		55,000	
Profit from operations	64,000		73,800	

70

Task 11.5

Fissie Drinks Ltd had budgeted to manufacture and sell 30,000 cans of pop in January. However, due to a health scare in the media about pop, it was only able to manufacture and sell 25,000 cans. Fissie Drinks Ltd's manufacturing costs are all variable except for fixed overheads.

(a) **Complete the table below to show a flexed budget and the resulting variances against the budget for January. Show the actual variance amount for sales revenue and each cost in the column headed 'Variance'.**

Note:

- **Adverse variances must be denoted with a minus sign or brackets.**

- **Enter 0 where any figure is zero.**

	Original budget	Flexed budget	Actual	Variance
Number of cans	30,000	25,000	25,000	
	£	£	£	£
Sales revenue	22,500		18,000	
Less costs:				
Direct materials and direct labour	10,500		8,500	
Variable overheads	6,000		4,200	
Fixed overheads	4,000		4,100	
Profit from operations	2,000		1,200	

(b) Referring to your answer for part (a), which one of the variances has had the greatest impact in increasing the profit from operations?

	✓
Sales revenue	
Direct materials and direct labour	
Variable overheads	
Fixed overheads	

(c) Which one of the following might have caused the variance for direct materials and direct labour costs?

	✓
A decrease in material prices	
An increase in employees' pay	
An increase in material prices	
Less efficient usage of direct labour	

Chapter 12 – Cost bookkeeping

Task 12.1

Drag and drop the correct entries into the journal below to record the following transactions:

1   Production overheads absorbed into production
2   Indirect labour transferred to production overheads
3   Completed WIP transferred to finished goods
4   Direct materials issued to production

The choices are:

Debit: WIP, Credit: Production overheads

Debit: Production overheads, Credit: Wages

Debit: Finished goods, Credit: WIP

Debit: WIP, Credit: Materials

Debit: WIP, Credit: Finished goods

Debit: Production overheads, Credit: WIP

Production overheads absorbed into production		
Indirect labour transferred to production overheads		
Completed WIP transferred to finished goods		
Direct materials issued to production		

Task 12.2

Drag and drop the correct entries into the journal below to record the following transactions for overheads:

Transaction 1.   Over-absorbed: absorbed greater than incurred
Transaction 2.   Under-absorbed: incurred greater than absorbed

The drag and drop choices are:

- Debit: production overheads, Credit: statement of profit or loss
- Debit: statement of profit or loss, Credit: production overheads

	Drag and drop choice
Transaction 1	
Transaction 2	

Task 12.3

A company operates an integrated accounting system.

The accounting entries for the issue to production of indirect materials from inventory would be:

Debit	Credit	✓
Work in progress account	Materials control account	
Materials control account	Production overhead control account	
Production overhead control account	Materials control account	
Cost of sales account	Materials control account	

Task 12.4

Lol Ltd makes wooden bird boxes. Below are extracts from Lol Ltd's payroll for last week.

Date	Labour costs
8 June	Box manufacture: Production employees' pay 380 hours at £15 per hour
10 June	Box painting: Production employees' basic pay £2,100 + £250 overtime
12 June	Warehouse department Employees' pay £1,400 + 15% bonus
14 June	General Administration department: Staff salaries £3,400 + 20% bonus

Complete the cost journal entries to record the four payroll payments made last week.

Date	Code	Debit £	Credit £
8 June	▼		
8 June	▼		
10 June	▼		
10 June	▼		
12 June	▼		
12 June	▼		
14 June	▼		
14 June	▼		

Picklist:

OH01 Operating overheads
DI02 Box painting direct costs
OH02 Non-operating overheads
DI01 Box manufacture direct costs
WA01 Wages control account

Task 12.5

In JKR Ltd, the overhead for the period was under absorbed.

The accounting entries at the end of a period for production overhead under-absorbed would be **(tick the correct boxes)**:

	Debit	Credit	No entry in this a/c
Overhead control account			
Work in progress account			
Statement of profit or loss			

Chapter 13 – Marginal costing

Task 13.1

Paris Ltd uses absorption costing, but is looking at adopting marginal costing across some of its products. The details for the PA121 are below:

Direct materials	£8.50
Direct labour	£17.00
Variable overheads	£3.00
Fixed overheads	£850,000

Overheads are absorbed on the machine hour basis, and it is estimated that in the next accounting period machine hours will total 250,000. Each unit requires two hours of machine time.

What is the cost per unit using:

(a)   Absorption costing
(b)   Marginal costing?
....

Task 13.2

Drag and drop the correct answer into the sentence below:

Less for absorption costing
More for absorption costing
The same for both types of costing

In the long run, total profit for a company will be ⬚ whether marginal costing or absorption costing is used.
....

Task 13.3

Drag and drop the correct answer into the sentence below:

Absorption costing, marginal costing
Marginal costing, absorption costing

It might be argued that ⬚ is preferable to ⬚ **in management accounting**, in order to be consistent with the requirement of current accounting standards and financial reporting.
....

Task 13.4

Cost and selling price details for product Z are as follows.

	£
Direct materials	6.00
Direct labour	7.50
Variable overhead	2.50
Fixed overhead absorption rate	5.00
	21.00
Profit	9.00
Selling price	30.00

Budgeted production for the month was 5,000 units although the company managed to produce 5,800 units, selling 5,200 of them and incurring fixed overhead costs of £27,400.

(a) What was the marginal costing profit for the month?

	✓
£45,400	
£46,800	
£53,800	
£72,800	

(b) What was the absorption costing profit for the month?

	✓
£45,200	
£45,400	
£46,800	
£48,400	

Task 13.5

Product Dee is made in batches of 16,000 units and the following costs are estimated.

Product Dee	£ per batch
Direct materials	176,000
Direct labour	230,400
Variable overheads	48,000
Fixed manufacturing overheads	73,600
Fixed administration, selling and distribution costs	54,400
Total costs	582,400

(a) **Calculate the total cost of one unit of product Dee.**

£ [   ]

(b) **Calculate the full absorption cost of one unit of product Dee.**

£ [   ]

(c) **Calculate the full absorption cost of one batch of product Dee.**

£ [   ]

(d) **Calculate the marginal cost of one batch of product Dee.**

£ [   ]

(e) **Calculate the marginal cost of one unit of product Dee.**

£ [   ]

Task 14.1

The COLIN has a selling price of £22 per unit with a total variable cost of £17 per unit. Paris Ltd estimates that the fixed costs per quarter associated with this product are £45,000.

(a) **Calculate the budgeted breakeven, in units, for product COLIN.**

	units

(b) **Calculate the budgeted breakeven sales, in £s, for product COLIN.**

£	

(c) **Complete the table below to show the budgeted margin of safety in units and the margin of safety percentage (to the nearest whole %) and the margin of safety in revenue if Paris Ltd sells 9,500 units or 10,500 units of product COLIN.**

Units of COLIN sold	9,500	10,500
Margin of safety (units)		
Margin of safety percentage		
Margin of safety revenue		

(d) **If Paris Ltd wishes to make a profit of £20,000, how many units of COLIN must it sell?**

	units

(e) **If Paris Ltd increases the selling price of COLIN by £1 what will be the impact on the breakeven point and the margin of safety, assuming no change in the number of units sold?**

	✓
The breakeven point will decrease and the margin of safety will increase.	
The margin of safety will stay the same but the breakeven point will increase.	
The breakeven point will decrease and the margin of safety will stay the same.	
The margin of safety will decrease and the breakeven point will decrease.	

Task 14.2

(a) Paris Ltd has decided to limit the production of the COLIN to 8,000 units per quarter. If the selling price and variable costs remain the same, what is the maximum fixed costs per quarter to breakeven? Remember the selling price is £22 per unit and the variable cost is £17 per unit.

(b) Calculate the revised budgeted breakeven, in £s, for product COLIN if fixed costs are £30,000 per quarter.

£ [   ]

(c) Complete the table below to show the budgeted margin of safety in units and the margin of safety percentage (to the nearest whole %) if Paris Ltd sells 6,500 units or 7,000 units of product COLIN. Base this on your answer in part (b).

Units of COLIN sold	6,500	7,000
	£	£
Margin of safety (units)		
Margin of safety percentage		

(d) If Paris Ltd wishes to make a profit of £10,000, how many units of COLIN must it sell? Is it possible to make this level of profit? Base this on the data in parts (a), (b) and (c).

[   ] units

Task 14.3

A company makes a single product and incurs fixed costs of £30,000 per month. Variable cost per unit is £5 and each unit sells for £15. Monthly sales demand is 7,000 units.

The breakeven point in terms of monthly sales units is:

	✓
2,000 units	
3,000 units	
4,000 units	
6,000 units	

Task 14.4

A company manufactures a single product for which cost and selling price data are as follows.

Selling price per unit   £12

Variable cost per unit   £8

Fixed costs per month   £96,000

Budgeted monthly sales   30,000 units

The margin of safety, expressed as a percentage of budgeted monthly sales, is (to the nearest whole number):

	✓
20%	
25%	
73%	
125%	

Task 14.5

Information concerning K Co's single product is as follows.

	£ per unit
Selling price	6.00
Variable production cost	1.20
Variable selling cost	0.40
Fixed production cost	4.00
Fixed selling cost	0.80

Budgeted production and sales for the year are 10,000 units.

(a) **What is the company's breakeven point, to the nearest whole unit?**

	✓
8,000 units	
8,333 units	
10,000 units	
10,909 units	

(b) **How many units must be sold if K Co wants to achieve a profit of £11,000 for the year?**

	✓
2,500 units	
9,833 units	
10,625 units	
13,409 units	

Task 14.6

Bluetop Ltd is reviewing two contracts, Top4 and Top5, for next month. The contracts will require a specialist grade of material. The following forecasts have been prepared:

Forecast	Top4	Top5	Total
Contribution (£)	18,000	13,500	31,500
Fixed costs (£)	5,000	5,000	10,000
Profit from operations (£)	13,000	8,500	21,500
Number of units	3,000	1,500	
Total specialist material required (kg)	1,125	750	

There is a shortage of specialist material for next month due to a supplier shortage.

This means that only 1,125 kg of specialist material is expected to be available for these two contracts.

(a) **Complete all cells in the forecast profit statement below to recommend how many units should be produced under each contract, and the forecast profit/loss made.**

Forecast	Top4	Top5	Total
Contribution per unit (£)			
Contribution per kg (£)			
Ranking			
Total material available (kg)			
Material allocated (kg)			
Number of units produced			
Total contribution earned (£)			
Less: fixed costs (£)			
Forecast profit/loss made (£)			

(b) **Complete the following sentence, using your results from (a) above.**

Contract Top5 [▼] be selected as the first contract to produce

next month as it has the highest [▼] .

Picklist:

should
should not
contribution per unit
contribution per kg used

Task 14.7

Golden Ltd is reviewing two contracts, Sun and Rain, for next month. The contracts will require a specialist grade of labour. The following forecasts have been prepared:

Forecast	Sun	Rain
Contribution (£)	9,000	6,000
Fixed costs (£)	3,500	3,500
Profit from operations (£)	5,500	2,500
Number of units	3,000	1,500
Total specialist labour hours required (hours)	2,250	3,000

There is a shortage of specialist labour for next month due to staff holidays.

This means that only 5,000 hours of specialist labour are expected to be available for these two contracts.

Complete all cells in the forecast profit statement below to recommend how many units should be produced under each contract, and the forecast profit/loss made.

Forecast	Sun	Rain	Total
Contribution per unit (£)			
Contribution per hour (£)			
Ranking			
Total labour hours available (hours)			
Labour hours allocated (hours)			
Number of units produced			
Total contribution earned (£)			
Less: fixed costs (£)			
Forecast profit/loss made (£)			

Chapter 15 – Long-term decision making

Task 15.1

Beanie Ltd has a stamping machine nearing the end of its useful life and is considering purchasing a replacement machine.

Estimates have been made for the initial capital cost, sales income and operating costs of the replacement machine, which is expected to have a useful life of four years:

	Year 0 £000	Year 1 £000	Year 2 £000	Year 3 £000	Year 4 £000
Capital expenditure	1,000				
Other cash flows:					
Sales income		350	400	400	350
Operating costs		100	110	120	130

The company appraises capital investment projects using a 11% cost of capital.

(a) **Complete the table below and calculate the net present value of the proposed replacement machine (to the nearest £'000):**

	Year 0 £000	Year 1 £000	Year 2 £000	Year 3 £000	Year 4 £000
Capital expenditure					
Sales income					
Operating costs					
Net cash flows					
PV factors	1.0000	0.9009	0.8116	0.7312	0.6587
Discounted cash flows (to nearest £)					
Net present value					

The net present value is [ ] ▼ .

Picklist:

positive
negative

(b) **Calculate the payback period of the proposed replacement machine to the nearest whole month.**

The payback period is [ ] year(s) and [ ] month(s).

Task 15.2

The Managing Director of Beanie Ltd has been looking at your calculations for the replacement machine. **He wants to know the maximum he should pay for a replacement machine to make sure the NPV at least breaks even.**

£ [ ]

Task 15.3

It has now been decided to purchase the replacement stamping machine, but the managing director wants you to use a lower rate for the cost of capital and he has settled on 7%. He also wants you to use a figure of £810,000 for the cost of the replacement machine. All other cash flows are as before.

	Year 0 £000	Year 1 £000	Year 2 £000	Year 3 £000	Year 4 £000
Capital expenditure	810				
Other cash flows:					
Sales income		350	400	400	350
Operating costs		100	110	120	130

The company appraises capital investment projects using a 7% cost of capital.

Complete the table below and calculate the net present value of the proposed replacement machine (to the nearest £000):

	Year 0 £000	Year 1 £000	Year 2 £000	Year 3 £000	Year 4 £000
Capital expenditure					
Sales income					
Operating costs					
Net cash flows					
PV factors	1.0000	0.9346	0.8734	0.8163	0.7629
Discounted cash flows (to nearest £)					
Net present value					

The net present value is ☐ .

Picklist:

positive
negative

Task 15.4

A Ltd is thinking of investing in Project B.

(a) **Complete the table below to calculate the net present value of Project B, rounding to the nearest whole £. You MUST use minus signs where appropriate.**

	Year 0 £	Year 1 £	Year 2 £	Year 3 £	Year 4 £
Net cash flows	−180,000	42,000	50,000	75,000	80,000
PV factors (15%)	1.000	0.8696	0.7561	0.6575	0.5718
Discounted cash flow					
NPV					

(b) Project B is also to be evaluated using a cost of capital of 10%.

Complete the table below to calculate the net present value of Project B, rounding to the nearest whole £. You MUST use minus signs where appropriate.

	Year 0 £	Year 1 £	Year 2 £	Year 3 £	Year 4 £
Net cash flows	−180,000	42,000	50,000	75,000	80,000
PV factors (10%)	1.000	0.9090	0.8264	0.7513	0.6830
Discounted cash flow					
NPV					

(c) **What is the approximate internal rate of return (IRR) of the project?**

	✓
0%	
10%	
12.5%	
15%	

Task 15.5

A project has the following NPVs at various costs of capital.

Cost of capital	NPV £
7%	20,255
9%	12,515
11%	5,395

What is the approximate IRR of the project?

	✓
0%	
7.4%	
10%	
11.4%	

Task 15.6

A project has the following NPVs at the following discount rates.

Discount rate %	NPV £
12	6,000
14	-3,000

What is the approximate IRR of the project?

	✓
1.3%	
12.7%	
13.3%	
16.0%	

Task 15.7

Several projects have the following NPVs and payback periods.

Project	NPV £	Payback
A	23,000	2.4
B	46,000	3.5
C	14,000	2.6
D	30,000	3.2

If the business is most interested in the return offered by the project, which project should be chosen?

	✓
Project A	
Project B	
Project C	
Project D	

Task 15.8

Several projects have the following NPVs and payback periods.

Project	NPV £	Payback years
A	23,000	2.4
B	46,000	3.5
C	14,000	2.6
D	30,000	3.2

If the business is most interested in limiting the risk offered by the project, which project should be chosen?

	✓
Project A	
Project B	
Project C	
Project D	

....

Task 15.9

Review the statements in the box below and identify whether they are true or not by selecting the correct options.

Statement	True	False
If the cost of capital is greater than the IRR for a project, then the project is worthwhile.		
The IRR is the discount rate which gives a zero NPV.		
The payback method uses cash flows from a project to determine the payback period.		
The shorter the payback period of a project, the lower the risk.		

....

Answer Bank

Chapter 1

Task 1.1

	Financial accounting	Management accounting
Users	External to the organisation	Internal management
Timing	Annual	When required
Type of information	Historic	Historic and future
Format	Specified by law	To be useful

Task 1.2

Cost card	£
Direct Materials	X
Direct labour	X
Direct expenses	X
Prime cost	X
Production overheads	X
Production cost	X
Non-production overheads	
– selling and distribution	X
– administration	X
– finance	X
Total cost	X

Task 1.3

The correct answer is: Costs and revenues

Profit centre managers are normally responsible for costs and revenues only.

Task 1.4

The correct answer is: The total of direct costs

Prime cost is the total of direct material, direct labour and direct expenses.

All costs incurred in manufacturing a product describes total production cost, including absorbed production overhead. **The material cost of a product** is only a part of prime cost.

Task 1.5

Cost card – toy soldier	£
Direct materials Wood and paint	3.50
Direct labour Toy maker's wages	3.00
Direct expenses Hire of special tools	0.50
Prime cost	7.00
Rent, rates, heat and light	0.30
Production cost	7.30
Non-production overheads:	
Advertising and sales promotion	0.70
Total cost	8.00

Task 1.6

Description	Principle
Complying with relevant laws and regulations	Professional behaviour
Not disclosing information to third parties without authority	Confidentiality
Being straightforward and honest in all professional and business relationships	Integrity
Not allowing bias or conflict of interest	Objectivity
Maintaining professional knowledge and skill	Professional competence and due care

Task 1.7

The correct answer is: The costs relating to a component of the business which generates revenue.

Chapter 2

Task 2.1

Cost types	
Production cost	**Factory heat and light**
	Depreciation of plant and machinery
Selling and distribution cost	**Sales Director's salary**
	Depreciation of delivery vans
	Fuel and oil for delivery vans
Administration cost	**Finance Director's salary**

Task 2.2

The correct answer is: A maintenance assistant in a factory maintenance department.

The maintenance assistant is not working directly on the organisation's output but is performing an indirect task. All the other three options describe tasks that involve working directly on the output.

Task 2.3

The correct answer is: Staples to fix the fabric to the seat of a chair

Indirect costs are those which **cannot be easily identified** with a specific cost unit. Although the staples could probably be identified with a specific chair, the cost is likely to be relatively insignificant. The expense of tracing such costs does not usually justify the possible benefits from calculating more accurate direct costs. The cost of the staples would therefore be treated as an indirect cost, to be included as a part of the overhead absorption rate.

The other options all represent significant costs which can be traced to a specific cost unit. Therefore they are classified as direct costs.

Task 2.4

The correct answer is: A selling and distribution overhead. The deliveries occur after a sale is made, therefore drivers' wages are a selling and distribution overhead.

Task 2.5

Carbon for racquet heads	**Direct material**
Office stationery	**Administration costs**
Wages of employees stringing racquets	**Direct labour**
Supervisors' salaries	**Indirect labour**
Advertising stand at badminton tournaments	**Selling and distribution costs**

Task 2.6

Graph A – variable cost per unit

Graph B – total fixed cost across level of activity

Task 2.7

	Output (units)	Total cost £
Highest	26,500	410,000
Lowest	16,000	252,500
Increase	10,500	157,500

Variable cost per unit = 157,500/10,500 = £15 per unit

Fixed cost

16,000 × £15	= £240,000
£252,500 – £240,000	= £12,500

OR

26,500 × £15	=	£397,500
£410,000 − £397,500	=	£12,500

Task 2.8

The correct answer is Graph 2. Graph 2 shows that costs increase in line with activity levels.

Task 2.9

The correct answer is Graph 1. Graph 1 shows that fixed costs remain the same whatever the level of activity.

Task 2.10

The correct answer is Graph 1. Graph 1 shows that cost per unit remains the same at different levels of activity.

Task 2.11

The correct answer is Graph 4. Graph 4 shows that semi-variable costs have a fixed element and a variable element.

Task 2.12

The correct answer is Graph 3. Graph 3 shows that the step fixed costs go up in 'steps' as the level of activity increases.

Task 2.13

The correct answer is: £5,100

	Units	£
High output	1,100	18,300
Low output	700	13,500
Variable cost	400	4,800

Variable cost per unit £4,800/400 = £12 per unit

Fixed costs = £18,300 − (£12 × 1,100) = £5,100

Therefore the correct answer is £5,100.

£13,500 is the total cost for an activity of 700 units

£13,200 is the total variable cost for 1,100 units (1,100 × £12)

£4,800 is the difference between the costs incurred at the two activity levels recorded

Task 2.14

The correct answer is variable. In the long run, all costs are variable.

Task 2.15

The correct answer is: £ 76,000

	£
Variable costs 8,000 × £8	64,000
Fixed costs	12,000
	76,000

Chapter 3

Task 3.1

(a) The EOQ is 600 kg = $\sqrt{\dfrac{[2 \times 90,000 \times 2]}{1}}$

(b) and (c) Inventory record card – FIFO

Date	Receipts Quantity kg	Cost per kg £	Total cost £	Issues Quantity kg	Cost per kg £	Total cost £	Balance Quantity kg	Total cost £
Balance as at 22 September							150	180
24 September	600	1.398	839				750	1,019
26 September				400	1.325	530	350	489
28 September	600	1.402	841				950	1,330
30 September				500	1.398	699	450	631

Note that the cost of the 400 kg issued on 26 September is made up of

$\quad$ 150 kg @ £1.20 $\quad$ = £180

$\quad$ <u>250</u> kg @ £1.398 = <u>£350</u>

Total $\quad$ 400 kg $\qquad\qquad$ = £530 $\qquad$ So the cost per kg = £530 ÷ 400 kg = 1.325

Note that the cost of the 500 kg issued on 30 September is made up of

$\quad$ 350 kg @ £1.398 = £489

$\quad$ <u>150</u> kg @ £1.402 = <u>£210</u>

Total $\quad$ 500 kg $\qquad\qquad$ = £699 $\qquad$ So the cost per kg = £699 ÷ 500 kg = 1.398

Task 3.2

Inventory record card

	Receipts			Issues			Balance	
Date	Quantity kg	Cost per kg £	Total cost £	Quantity kg	Cost per kg £	Total cost £	Quantity kg	Total cost £
Balance as at 1 January							4,000	10,000
31 January	1,000	2.0	2,000				5,000	12,000
15 February				3,000	2.5	7,500	2,000	4,500
28 February	1,500	2.5	3,750				3,500	8,250
14 March				500	2.5	1,250	3,000	7,000

Task 3.3

Inventory record card – AVCO

	Inventory Record Card							
	Purchases			Requisitions			Balance	
Date	Quantity kg	Cost £	Total cost £	Quantity kg	Cost £	Total cost £	Quantity kg	Total cost £
1 Jan							300	7,500
2 Jan				250	25.00	6,250	50	1,250
12 Jan	400	25.75	10,300				450	11,550
21 Jan				200	25.67	5,134	250	6,416
29 Jan				75	25.67	1,925	175	4,491

Task 3.4

	Receipts			Issues			Balance	
Date	Quantity kg	Cost per kg £	Total cost £	Quantity kg	Cost per kg £	Total cost £	Quantity kg	Total cost £
1 January	4,000	2.50	10,000				4,000	10,000
31 January	1,000	2.00	2,000				5,000	12,000
15 February				3,000	2.50	7,500	2,000	4,500
28 February	1,500	2.50	3,750				3,500	8,250
14 March				500	2.50	1,250	3,000	7,000

Task 3.5

Date	Receipts			Issues			Balance	
	Quantity	Cost per kg	Total cost	Quantity	Cost per kg	Total cost	Quantity	Total cost
	kg	£	£	kg	£	£	kg	£
1 January	4,000	2.50	10,000				4,000	10,000
31 January	1,000	2.00	2,000				5,000	12,000
15 February				3,000	2.33	7,000	2,000	5,000
28 February	1,500	2.50	3,750				3,500	8,750
14 March				500	2.50	1,250	3,000	7,500

Note that the cost of the 3,000 kg issued on 15 February is made up of

1,000 kg @ £2.00	=	£2,000
2,000 kg @ £2.50	=	£5,000
Total 3,000 kg	=	£7,000

So the cost per kg = £7,000 ÷ 3,000 kg = £2.33 and this gives a rounding difference in the table above because 3,000 kg × £2.33 = £6,990 rather than £7,000.

••

Task 3.6

	Cost £
AVCO issue	£19,890
FIFO issue	£16,205
LIFO issue	£22,937
AVCO balance	£33,462
FIFO balance	£37,147
LIFO balance	£30,415

£23,275   £14,455

Workings

AVCO cost per unit = (£15,960 + £23,520 + £13,872)/(840 + 960 + 480) = £53,352/2,280) = £23.40

AVCO issue cost of 850 units = £23.40 × 850 = £19,890

FIFO issue cost of 850 units = 840 units at £19 and 10 units at £24.50 = £15,960 + (10 units × £24.50) = £16,205

LIFO issue cost of 850 units = 480 units at £28.90 and (850 – 480) units at £24.50 = £13,872 + (370 × £24.50) = £22,937

AVCO closing balance = (840 + 960 + 480 – 850) × £23.40 = £33,462

FIFO closing balance = ((960 – 10) × £24.50) + £13,872 = £37,147

LIFO closing balance = (590 × £24.50) + £15,960 = £30,415

Task 3.7

The economic order quantity is $\boxed{300}$ units.

The formula for the economic order quantity (EOQ) is

$$EOQ = \sqrt{\frac{2cd}{h}}$$

With

c   = £10

d   = 5,400

h   = £0.10 × 12 months = £1.20

$$EOQ = \sqrt{\frac{2 \times £10 \times 5,400}{£1.20}}$$

$$= \sqrt{90,000}$$

$$= 300 \text{ units}$$

Task 3.8

The economic order quantity is $\boxed{175}$ units (to the nearest whole unit).

$$EOQ = \sqrt{\frac{2cd}{h}}$$

$$= \sqrt{\frac{2 \times £100 \times 1,225}{£8}}$$

$$= \sqrt{30,625}$$

$$= 175 \text{ units}$$

Task 3.9

The maximum inventory level was ⎡ 6,180 ⎤ units

Reorder level = maximum usage × maximum lead time

= 130 × 26 = 3,380 units

Maximum level = reorder level + reorder quantity – (minimum usage × minimum lead time)

= 3,380 + 4,000 – (60 × 20)

= 6,180 units.

Task 3.10

Statement	True ✓	False ✓
Issues of inventory using first in, first out (FIFO) will always be costed at the latest purchase price.		✓
Just-in-time (JIT) involves keeping inventory levels to a minimum.	✓	
Just-in-time (JIT) depends on having reliable suppliers.	✓	

Chapter 4

Task 4.1

Employee's weekly timesheet for week ending 14 May

Employee: H. Hector				Cost Centre: Lipsy calibration			
Employee number: LP100				**Basic pay per hour:** £9.00			

	Hours spent on production	Hours worked on indirect work	Notes	Basic pay £	Overtime premium £	Total pay £
Monday	6	1	10am–11am setting up of machinery	63	0	63
Tuesday	3	4	9am–1pm department meeting	63	0	63
Wednesday	8			72	3	75
Thursday	8			72	3	75
Friday	6	1	3pm–4pm health and safety training	63	0	63
Saturday	4			36	9	45
Sunday	4			36	36	72
Total	**39**	**6**		405	51	456

Task 4.2

Employee's weekly timesheet for week ending 14 May

Employee: H. Hector				Cost Centre: Lipsy calibration		
Employee number: LP100				Basic pay per hour: £10.00		
	Hours spent on production	Hours worked on indirect work	Notes	Basic pay £	Overtime premium £	Total pay £
Monday	6	1	10am–11am setting up of machinery	70	0	70
Tuesday	3	4	9am–1pm department meeting	70	0	70
Wednesday	8			80	2.50	82.50
Thursday	8			80	2.50	82.50
Friday	6	1	3pm–4pm health and safety training	70	0	70
Saturday	4			40	0	40
Sunday	4			40	20	60
Total	39	6		450	25	475

Task 4.3

These details are recorded in the wages control account as follows:

Wages control account

	£		£
Bank	250,000	WIP	275,000
HM Revenue & Customs	62,500	Production overhead control	75,000
Welfare scheme contributions	37,500		
	350,000		350,000

Task 4.4

Work in progress control account

		£			£
31 May	Wages control	275,000			

Production overhead control

		£			£
31 May	Wages control	75,000			

Task 4.5

The correct answer is: Maintenance workers in a shoe factory. Maintenance workers will not be involved in actually making the shoes. Machinists in a clothes manufacturer will be involved in making the clothes and are therefore direct labour. Bricklayers actually make the buildings so are also direct labour.

Task 4.6

	✓
DEBIT Wages control CREDIT Overhead control	
DEBIT Admin overhead control CREDIT Wages control	
DEBIT Overhead control CREDIT Wages control	✓
DEBIT Wages control CREDIT Admin overhead control	

Indirect wages are 'collected' in the overhead control account, for subsequent absorption into work in progress.

Task 4.7

	Code	Dr £	Cr £
Manufacturing department A wages	2300	18,500	
Manufacturing department A wages	6000		18,500
Manufacturing department B wages	2400	22,500	
Manufacturing department B wages	6000		22,500
Maintenance department wages	3400	12,700	
Maintenance department wages	6000		12,700
General admin department salaries	3500	7,600	
General admin department salaries	6000		7,600

Task 4.8

			✓
DEBIT Wages control	CREDIT	Work in progress account	
DEBIT Work in progress account	CREDIT	Wages control	✓
DEBIT Costs of sales account	CREDIT	Work in progress account	
DEBIT Finished goods account	CREDIT	Work in progress account	

The **direct costs of production**, of which direct wages are a part, are **debited to the work in progress account**. The credit entry is made in the **wages control account**, where the wages cost has been 'collected' **prior to its analysis** between direct and indirect wages.

....

Task 4.9

(a) **Employee's weekly timesheet for week ending 7 December**

	Hours	Total pay £
Basic pay (including basic hours for overtime)	48	720.00
Mon–Fri overtime premium	7	52.50
Sat–Sun overtime premium	6	90.00
Total		862.50

(b) | £ | 135 |
|---|---|

£15 × 30% = £4.50 per unit

30 extra units × £4.50 = £135

(c) | 4,200 | units

7,000 units × 60% = 4,200 units

....

Task 4.10

£	0.325

$$\frac{£13,650}{42,000} = £0.325$$

....

Task 4.11

(a)

Labour cost	Hours	Workings	£
Basic pay	800	800 × £22.00	17,600
Overtime rate 1	50	50 × £33.00	1,650
Overtime rate 2	40	40 × £44.00	1,760
Total cost before bonus	890	890	21,010
Bonus payment		(600 × £8.80)	5,280
Total cost including bonus			26,290

(b) The total labour cost of producing each unit in the month of April is:

£	8.80

£26,290/2,987.50 = £8.80

(c) The basic pay and overtime for each member of department B for April was:

£	5,252.50

and the bonus payable to each team member was:

£	1,320

£21,010/4 = £5,252.50

£5,280/4 = £1,320

....

Chapter 5

Task 5.1

	Basis of apportionment	Silicon moulding £	Silicon extrusion £	Maintenance £	Stores £	General Admin £	Totals £
Depreciation of plant and equipment	NBV of plant and equipment	904,669	1,105,706				2,010,375
Power for production machinery	Production machinery power usage (KwH)	572,500	1,215,000				1,787,500
Rent and rates	Floor space			74,648	93,310	93,310	261,268
Light and heat	Floor space			16,500	20,625	20,625	57,750
Indirect labour	Allocated			253,750	90,125	600,251	944,126
Totals		1,477,169	2,320,706	344,898	204,060	714,186	5,061,019
Reapportion Maintenance		120,714	224,184	(344,898)			
Reapportion Stores		81,624	122,436		(204,060)		
Reapportion General Admin		357,093	357,093			(714,186)	
Total overheads to production centres		2,036,600	3,024,419				5,061,019

Task 5.2

(a)

	Basis of apportionment	Silicon moulding £	Silicon extrusion £	Maintenance £	Stores £	General Admin £	Totals £
Depreciation of plant and equipment	Headcount	972,762	1,037,613				2,010,375
Power for production machinery	Headcount	864,919	922,581				1,787,500
Rent and rates	Floor space			74,648	93,310	93,310	261,268
Light and heat	Floor space			16,500	20,625	20,625	57,750
Indirect labour	Allocated			253,750	90,125	600,251	944,126
Totals		1,837,681	1,960,194	344,898	204,060	714,176	5,061,019
Reapportion Maintenance		120,714	224,184	(344,898)			
Reapportion Stores		81,624	122,436		(204,060)		
Reapportion General Admin		464,221	249,965			(714,186)	
Total overheads to production centres		2,504,240	2,556,779				5,061,019

(b) The manager would most likely argue with the revised basis of allocation as his/her costs have increased by £467,640. The use of headcount to apportion machinery costs is not common and the manager could argue that depreciation based on NBV, and power on consumption are better bases for reapportioning these costs. Nonetheless, if the cost centre is using more general admin then it is fair that it should bear more of that cost.

116

Task 5.3

£	16.50

The full absorption cost of a unit of Em excludes the fixed administration, selling and distribution costs.

£18.20 – £1.70 = £16.50

Task 5.4

Reapportionment – inter-service centre work is ignored here.

Direct method

	Production		Service centres		
	X	Y	Stores	Maintenance	General administration overheads
	£	£	£	£	£
Overheads	80,000	50,000	40,000	30,000	8,000
Reapportion Stores (55% and 45%)	22,000	18,000	(40,000)		
Reapportion Maintenance (8,000/ 15,000) and (7,000/ 15,000)	16,000	14,000		(30,000)	
Reapportion General admin overheads (50:50)	4,000	4,000			(8,000)
Total	122,000	86,000			

Task 5.5

Step-down method – inter-service work is taken into account in the first step only.

	Production		Service centres	
	X	Y	Stores	Maintenance
	£	£	£	£
Allocated overhead	80,000	50,000	40,000	30,000
Apportion stores (50:30:20)	20,000	12,000	(40,000)	8,000
				38,000
Apportion maintenance (30:50)	14,250	23,750		(38,000)
Total	114,250	85,750		

●●

Chapter 6

Task 6.1

(a)

	Silicon moulding	Silicon extrusion
Actual direct labour hours	21,222	17,144
Actual machine hours	8,459	6,501
Budgeted overhead absorbed – labour hrs	424,440	342,880
Budgeted overhead absorbed – machine hrs	465,245	357,555

(b)

	Silicon moulding	Silicon extrusion
Actual overheads (£)	425,799	354,416
Difference – labour hrs	1,359	11,536
Difference – machine hrs	39,446	3,139

Task 6.2

The correct answer is: Absorbed overheads exceed actual overheads.

Absorbed overheads exceeding budgeted overheads could lead to under-absorbed overheads if actual overheads far exceeded both budgeted overheads and the overhead absorbed. Actual overheads exceeding budgeted overheads could lead to under-absorbed overheads if overhead absorbed does not increase in line with actual overhead incurred.

Task 6.3

The correct answer is: £405,000

Budgeted absorption rate for fixed overhead = £360,000/8,000

= £45 per hour

Fixed overhead absorbed = 9,000 hours × £45

= £405,000

If you selected £384,000 you based your absorption calculations on sales units instead of labour hours.

If you selected £432,000 you calculated the correct figure for fixed overhead absorbed but also added the variable overheads.

£459,000 is the figure for actual total overhead incurred.

Task 6.4

The correct answer is: under-absorbed by £27,000

Actual fixed overhead incurred = £432,000

Fixed overhead absorbed = £405,000 (from Task 6.3)

Fixed overhead under absorbed = £27,000

If you selected under-absorbed by £72,000, you simply calculated the difference between the budgeted and actual fixed overhead. If you selected under-absorbed by £75,000, you based your absorption calculations on sales units instead of production units. If you selected over-absorbed by £27,000 you performed the calculations correctly but misinterpreted the result as an over absorption.

Task 6.5

Term	Description
Activity based costing	Identifying activities which cause costs to charge overheads to products
Cost driver	A factor influencing the level of cost
Cost pool	Equivalent to a cost centre in traditional absorption costing

Assigning only variable costs to cost units – refers to marginal costing

A cost which cannot be traced directly to a product – refers to an overhead

A unit of product for which costs can be ascertained – refers to a cost unit

Charging whole cost items direct to a cost unit – refers to allocation

Task 6.6

(a) The correct answer is: Silicon moulding £51/hour, Silicon extrusion £56/hour

(b) The correct answer is: Silicon moulding £18/hour, Silicon extrusion £17/hour

Task 6.7

	Silicon moulding	Silicon extrusion
Budgeted overheads (£)	450,000	352,520
Budgeted direct labour hours	22,500	17,626
Budgeted machine hours	8,182	6,409

Workings

£450,000/£20 = 22,500 labour hours

£352,520/£20 = 17,626 labour hours

£450,000/£55 = 8,182 machine hours

£352,520/£55 = 6,409 machine hours

Chapter 7

Task 7.1

Service	Cost unit
Road, rail and air transport services	Passenger/kilometre, tonne/kilometre
Hotels	Occupied bed-night
Education	Full-time student
Hospitals	Patient-day
Catering establishments	Meal served

Task 7.2

Job number 03456

	Budget £	Actual £	Variance F/A £
Direct materials			
Plasterboard	3,600.00	3,500.00	100F
Wood & door frames	4,750.00	4,802.00	52A
Insulation	1,050.00	1,145.00	95A
Electrical fittings	320.00	300.00	20F
Windows	2,220.00	2,576.00	356A
Paint	270.00	250.00	20F
Direct labour			
Construction	554.00	641.00	87A
Electrical	224.00	160.00	64F
Decorating	165.00	205.00	40A

	Budget £	Actual £	Variance F/A £
Direct expenses			
Hire of specialist lathe	240.00	240.00	0
Overheads (based upon direct labour hours)			
84/90 hours @ £15.00	1,260.00	1,350.00	90A

Task 7.3

(a) and (b)

	Budget £	Actual £	Variance F/A £	%
Direct materials				
Plasterboard	3,600.00	3,500.00	100F	2.8
Wood & door frames	4,750.00	4,802.00	52A	1.1
Insulation	1,050.00	1,145.00	95A	9.0
Electrical fittings	320.00	300.00	20F	6.3
Windows	2,220.00	2,576.00	356A	16.0
Paint	270.00	250.00	20F	7.4
Direct labour				
Construction	554.00	641.00	87A	15.7
Electrical	224.00	160.00	64F	28.6
Decorating	165.00	205.00	40A	24.2
Direct expenses				
Hire of specialist lathe	240.00	240.00	0	0

	Budget £	Actual £	Variance F/A £	%
Overheads (based upon direct labour hours)				
84/90 hours @ £15.00	1,260.00	1,350.00	90A	7.1
Total cost	14,653.00	15,169.00	516.00 A	
Profit	2,930.60	2,414.60		
Net price	17,583.60	17,583.60		
VAT at 20%	3,516.72	3,516.72		
Total price	21,100.32	21,100.32		

(c) (2,930.60 − 2,414.60)/2,930.60 = 17.6%

Task 7.4

	✓
High levels of indirect costs as a proportion of total cost	✓
Cost units are often intangible	✓
Use of composite cost units	✓
Use of equivalent units	

In service costing it is difficult to identify many attributable direct costs. Many costs must be treated as indirect costs and shared over several cost units, therefore there are high levels of indirect costs as a proportion of total cost. Many services are intangible, for example a haircut or a cleaning service provide no physical, tangible product. Composite cost units such as passenger-mile or bed-night are often used in service costing. 'Use of equivalent units' does not apply because equivalent units are more often used in costing for tangible products.

Task 7.5

(a)

£	18.20

$$\frac{582,400}{32,000} = £18.20$$

(b)

£	16.50

$$\frac{582,400 - 54,400}{32,000} = £16.50$$

(c)

£	528,000

£16.50 × 32,000 units = £528,000 or £582,400 − £54,400 = £528,000

Task 8.1

(a)

Description	Kg	Unit cost £	Total cost £	Description	Kg	Unit cost £	Total cost £
Material TL4	700	1.35	945	Normal loss	145	0.60	87
Material TL3	350	1.50	525	Output	1,305	6.66	8,691
Material TL9	400	1.25	500				
Labour			3,700				
Overheads			3,108				
	1,450		8,778		1,450		8,778

(b)

	Debit	Credit
Abnormal loss account	✓	
Process account		✓

Workings

Labour: 2 × 37 hours × 4 weeks × £12.50 = £3,700

Overheads: £10.50 × 2 × 37 hours × 4 weeks = £3,108

Unit cost = (£8,778 − £87)/1,305 = £6.66

Task 8.2

Description	Kg	Unit cost £	Total cost £	Description	Kg	Unit cost £	Total cost £
Material TL4	700	1.35	945	Normal loss	290	0.60	174
Material TL3	350	1.50	525	Output	1,160	7.07	8,196*
Material TL9	400	1.25	500				
Labour			3,040				
Overheads			3,360				
	1,450		8,370		1,450		8,370

* Note there is a rounding difference here.

The decision made to employ cheaper employees has resulted in the process costing more but higher losses are incurred too. However over time, the workers may get more efficient, taking less time and the losses may go down.

●●●

Task 8.3

The correct answer is 2,000 kg

Process account

	Debit		Credit
Opening WIP	4,500	Output	60,400
Input	54,300	Normal loss	400
Abnormal gain	2,000		–
	60,800		60,800

The abnormal gain is the balancing figure. 60,800 – 4,500 – 54,300 = 2,000

■■■

Task 8.4

The quantity of good production achieved was $\boxed{2{,}625}$ kg.

Good production = input – normal loss – abnormal loss

$$= 3{,}000 - (10\% \times 3{,}000) - 75$$
$$= 3{,}000 - 300 - 75$$
$$= \underline{2{,}625} \text{ kg}$$

Task 8.5

(a) The value credited to the process account for the scrap value of the normal will be £ $\boxed{100}$ to the nearest £.

Normal loss = 10% × input

$$= 10\% \times 5{,}000 \text{ kg}$$
$$= 500 \text{ kg}$$

When scrap has a value, normal loss is valued at the value of the scrap ie 20p per kg.

Normal loss = £0.20 × 500 kg

$$= £100$$

(b) The amount of abnormal loss for the period is 300 kg.

	Kg
Input	5,000
Normal loss (10% × 5,000 kg)	(500)
Abnormal loss	(300)
Output	4,200

Chapter 9

Task 9.1

	✓
A unit of output which is identical to all others manufactured in the same process	
Notional whole units used to represent uncompleted work	✓
A unit of product in relation to which costs are ascertained	
The amount of work achievable, at standard efficiency levels, in an hour	

An equivalent unit calculation is used in process costing to value any incomplete units within work in progress and losses.

The first option describes the output from any process, where all completed units are identical.

The third option describes a cost unit, and the fourth option describes a standard hour.

••

Task 9.2

We use equivalent units.

	Equivalent units
Completed production	20,400
Work in progress (8,000 × 25%)	2,000
	22,400

Therefore during the period the equivalent of 22,400 completed units have passed through the process. The cost per equivalent unit (EU) can now be found.

$$\text{Cost per equivalent unit} = \frac{£56,000}{22,400\,EU}$$

$$= £2.50 \text{ per equivalent unit}$$

••

Task 9.3

(a)

	Units	Materials		Labour/overheads	
		Proportion complete	Equivalent units	Proportion complete	Equivalent units
Completed	8,300	100%	8,300	100%	8,300
Work in progress	1,000	70%	700	60%	600
Total equivalent units			9,000		8,900
Cost per equivalent unit		=	£2.40 per EU	=	£1.50 per EU

Workings

Materials: Cost per equivalent unit = £21,600/9,000 units = £2.40

Labour: Cost per equivalent unit = £13,350/8,900 units = £1.50

(b)

	£
Completed output	
Materials (8,300 × £2.40)	19,920
Labour/overhead (8,300 × £1.50)	12,450
	32,370
Work in progress	
Materials (700 × £2.40)	1,680
Labour/overhead (600 × £1.50)	900
	2,580

Task 9.4

(a) FIFO

Unit calculation:

Opening + Input = Good output + Closing WIP
WIP   Units

	Actual	Equivalent Units		
	Units	Materials	Labour	Overheads
Opening WIP (W1)	100	–	40	70
Goods started and finished (= output – opening WIP)	3,940	3,940	3,940	3,940
Good output	4,040	3,940	3,980	4,010
Closing WIP (W2)	160	160	96	96
Equivalent units	4,200	4,100	4,076	4,106

Workings

1   Opening WIP is 100% complete for materials but 60% for labour and 30% for overheads.

    To complete – Labour (100 – 60)% = 40% × 100 = 40

                 – Overheads (100 – 30)% = 70% × 100 = 70

2   Closing WIP – 100% complete for materials so 100% × 160 = 160

                – 60% complete for labour so 60% × 160 = 96

                – 60% complete for overheads so 60% × 160 = 96

(b) Statement of cost per equivalent unit

	£	£	£
Input costs	45,100	32,608	16,424
Cost per equivalent unit = Input costs/Equivalent units	11.00	8.00	4.00

(c) Value of units

		£
Value of good output =	Costs b/f in opening WIP =	1,220
	Materials 3,940 × £11	43,340
	Labour 3,980 × £8	31,840
	Overheads 4,010 × £4	16,040
		92,440
Value of Closing WIP = 160 × £11 + 96 × £8 + 96 × £4 = £2,912		

(d) Process account

Process

	Units	£		Units	£
Opening WIP	100	1,220	Good output	4,040	92,440
Raw Materials	4,100	45,100	(see st of equiv units)		
Labour		32,608	Closing WIP (W2)	160	2,912
Overheads		16,424			
	4,200	95,352		4,200	95,352

Task 9.5

(a) Statement of equivalent units

	Actual	Equivalent units		
	Units	Materials	Labour	Overheads
Good output	4,040	4,040	4,040	4,040
Closing WIP	160	160	96	96
Equivalent units	4,200	4,200	4,136	4,136

(b) **Costs**

	£	£	£
Costs b/f (£1,220) (from the example)	800	360	60
Input costs	45,100	32,608	16,424
	45,900	32,968	16,484
Cost per equivalent unit = Input costs/Equivalent units	10.93	7.97	3.99
		Total £22.89	

(c) **Value of units**

Value of good output = £22.89 × 4,040 = £92,476
Value of Closing WIP = 160 × £10.93 + 96 × £7.97 + 96 × £3.99 = £2,897

(d) **Process account**

Process

	Units	£		Units	£
Opening WIP b/f	100	1,220	Output	4,040	92,476
Raw Materials	4,100	45,100	Closing WIP c/d	160	2,897
Labour		32,608			
Overheads		16,424	Rounding		(21)
	4,200	95,352		4,200	95,352

Chapter 10

Task 10.1

Batches produced and sold	3,000	3,750	5,000
	£	£	£
Sales revenue	60,000	75,000	100,000
Variable costs:			
Direct materials 1.90	5,700	7,125	9,500
Direct labour 9	27,000	33,750	45,000
Overheads 3.1	9,300	11,625	15,500
Semi-variable costs:	9,450		
Variable element		7,500	10,000
Fixed element		3,450	3,450
Total cost	51,450	63,450	83,450
Total profit	8,550	11,550	16,550
Profit per batch (to 2 decimal places)	2.85	3.08	3.31

Workings

Sales revenue	£60,000/3,000 batches = £20 per batch
Direct materials	£5,700/3,000 batches = £1.90 per batch
Direct labour	£27,000/3,000 batches = £9 per batch
Variable overheads	£9,300/3,000 batches = £3.1 per batch

(Note that the overheads are variable and therefore we calculate a cost per batch. If they were fixed overheads then the cost would be the same for 3,000 batches, 3,750 batches and 5,000 batches.)

Semi-variable cost 7,500   £18,450
                        7,000   £9,450

                         500   9,000

Variable cost = £9,000/500 = £2 per batch

Fixed cost = £18,450 – (7,500 × £2) = £3,450

Task 10.2

Batches produced and sold	3,000	3,750	5,000
	£	£	£
Sales revenue	60,000	75,000	100,000
Variable costs:			
Direct materials 2	6,000	7,500	10,000
Direct labour 10	30,000	37,500	50,000
Overheads 3.2	9,600	12,000	16,000
Semi-variable costs:	9,450		
Variable element		7,500	10,000
Fixed element		3,450	3,450
Total cost	55,050	67,950	89,450
Total profit	4,950	7,050	10,550
Profit per batch (to 2 decimal places)	1.65	1.88	2.11

Task 10.3

Batches produced and sold	3,000	4,000
	£	£
Sales revenue	60,000	80,000
Variable costs:		
Direct materials	6,000	8,000
Direct labour	30,000	40,000
Overheads	9,600	12,800
Semi-variable costs:		
Variable element	6,000	8,000
Fixed element	3,450	3,450
Total cost	55,050	72,250
Total profit	4,950	7,750
Profit per batch (to 2 decimal places)	1.65	1.94

Reject.

The profit per batch is less than £2 at 4,000 batches, so management should reject the order.

....

Task 10.4

Batches produced and sold	3,000	5,000	7,000
	£	£	£
Sales revenue	90,000	150,000	210,000
Variable costs:			
Direct materials	13,500	22,500	31,500
Direct labour	31,500	52,500	73,500
Overheads	18,000	30,000	42,000
Semi-variable costs:	9,450		
Variable element		10,000	14,000
Fixed element		3,450	3,450
Total cost	72,450	118,450	164,450
Total profit	17,550	31,550	45,550
Profit per batch (to 2 decimal places)	5.85	6.31	6.51

Task 10.5

Batches produced and sold	4,000	6,000	9,000
	£	£	£
Sales revenue	140,000	210,000	315,000
Variable costs:			
Direct materials	22,000	33,000	49,500
Direct labour	50,000	75,000	112,500
Overheads	28,000	42,000	63,000
Semi-variable costs:	16,750	22,750	31,750
Total cost	116,750	172,750	256,750
Total profit	23,250	37,250	58,250
Profit per batch (to 2 decimal places)	5.81	6.21	6.47

Chapter 11

Task 11.1

	Flexed Budget	Actual	Variance	Favourable F or Adverse A
Volume sold	156,000	156,000		
	£000	£000	£000	
Sales revenue	1,248	1,326	78	F
Less costs:				
Direct materials	390	372	18	F
Direct labour	468	444	24	F
Overheads	225	250	25	A
Operating profit	165	260	95	F

Task 11.2

	Flexed Budget	Actual	Budget unit cost/revenue	Actual unit cost/revenue
Volume sold	156,000	156,000		
	£000	£000		
Sales revenue	1,248	1,326	8	8.50
Less costs:				
Direct materials	390	372	2.50	2.38
Direct labour	468	444	3	2.85
Overheads	225	250		
Operating profit	165	260	1.06	1.67

They are all true. The unit selling price is higher than budgeted, which may be due to a rise in the sales price not planned for in the budget, or fewer bulk discounts to customers if these were planned for. The lower unit price for materials may arise from bulk buying discounts or new cheaper sources of supply. The lower labour costs may be due to a change in the make up of employees so there are more lower paid employees, or efficiency savings so fewer employees make the same number of units.

Task 11.3

	Original budget	Flexed budget	Actual	Variance
Number of packets	40,000	32,000	32,000	
	£	£	£	£
Sales revenue	130,000	104,000	96,000	–8,000
Less costs:				
Direct materials and direct labour	48,000	38,400	36,800	1,600
Variable overheads	22,000	17,600	19,200	–1,600
Fixed overheads	14,200	14,200	13,600	600
Profit from operations	45,800	33,800	26,400	

Task 11.4

	Original budget	Flexed budget	Actual	Variance
Number of books	60,000	45,000	45,000	
	£	£	£	£
Sales revenue	1,140,000	855,000	910,200	55,200
Less costs:				
Direct materials and direct labour	480,000	360,000	375,000	–15,000
Variable overheads	540,000	405,000	406,400	–1,400
Fixed overheads	56,000	56,000	55,000	1,000
Profit from operations	64,000	34,000	73,800	

Task 11.5

(a)

	Original budget	Flexed budget	Actual	Variance
Number of cans	30,000	25,000	25,000	
	£	£	£	£
Sales revenue	22,500	18,750	18,000	–750
Less costs:				
Direct materials and direct labour	10,500	8,750	8,500	250
Variable overheads	6,000	5,000	4,200	800
Fixed overheads	4,000	4,000	4,100	–100
Profit from operations	2,000	1,000	1,200	

(b) Referring to your answer for part (a), which one of the variances has had the greatest impact in increasing the profit from operations?

	✓
Sales revenue	
Direct materials and direct labour	
Variable overheads	✓
Fixed overheads	

(c) Which one of the following might have caused the variance for direct materials and direct labour costs?

	✓
A decrease in material prices	✓
An increase in employees' pay	
An increase in material prices	
Less efficient usage of direct labour	

Chapter 12

Task 12.1

Production overheads absorbed into production	Debit: WIP	Credit: Production overheads
Indirect labour transferred to production overheads	Debit: Production overheads	Credit: Wages
Completed WIP transferred to finished goods	Debit: Finished goods	Credit: WIP
Direct materials issued to production	Debit: WIP	Credit: Materials

Task 12.2

Drag and drop choice	
Transaction 1	Debit: production overheads, Credit: statement of profit or loss
Transaction 2	Debit: statement of profit or loss, Credit: production overheads

Task 12.3

The correct answer is: Debit: Production overhead control account, Credit: Materials control account

The cost of indirect materials issued is credited to the materials control account and 'collected' in the production overhead control account pending its absorption into work in progress.

Debit WIP account and Credit Materials control account represents the entries for the issue to production of **direct materials**.

Debit Cost of sales and Credit Materials control account is not correct. The issue of materials should not be charged direct to cost of sales. The cost of materials issued should first be analysed as direct or indirect and charged to work in progress or the overhead control account accordingly.

Task 12.4

Complete the cost journal entries to record the four payroll payments made last week.

Date	Code	Debit £	Credit £
8 June	DI01 Box manufacture direct costs	5,700	
8 June	WA01 Wages control account		5,700
10 June	DI02 Box painting direct costs	2,350	
10 June	WA01 Wages control account		2,350
12 June	OH01 Operating overheads	1,610	
12 June	WA01 Wages control account		1,610
14 June	OH02 Non-operating overheads	4,080	
14 June	WA01 Wages control account		4,080

Task 12.5

	Debit £	Credit £	No entry in this a/c £
Overhead control account		✓	
Work in progress account			✓
Statement of profit or loss	✓		

Under-absorbed overhead means that the overhead charged to production was too low and so there must be a debit to the statement of profit or loss.

Chapter 13

Task 13.1

(a) Absorption costing – unit cost

	£
Direct materials	8.50
Direct labour	17.00
Variable overheads	3.00
Prime cost	28.50
Fixed overheads ((£850,000/250,000) × 2)	6.80
Absorption cost	35.30

(b) Marginal costing – unit cost

	£
Direct materials	8.50
Direct labour	17.00
Variable overheads	3.00
Prime cost or marginal cost	28.50

Task 13.2

In the long run, total profit for a company will be │ the same for both types of costing │ whether marginal costing or absorption costing is used.

Task 13.3

It might be argued that │ absorption costing │ is preferable to │ marginal costing │ **in management accounting,** in order to be consistent with the requirement of current accounting standards and financial reporting.

Task 13.4

(a) £ | 45,400

		£	£
Sales	(5,200 × £30)		156,000
Direct materials	(5,800 × £6)	34,800	
Direct labour	(5,800 × £7.50)	43,500	
Variable overhead	(5,800 × £2.50)	14,500	
		92,800	
Less closing inventory	(600 × £16)	9,600	
			(83,200)
Contribution			72,800
Less fixed costs			27,400
			45,400

(b) £ | 48,400

		£	£
Sales	(5,200 × £30)		156,000
Materials	(5,800 × £6)	34,800	
Labour	(5,800 × £7.50)	43,500	
Variable overhead	(5,800 × £2.50)	14,500	
Fixed costs	(5,800 × £5)	29,000	
Less closing inventories	(600 × £21)	(12,600)	
			(109,200)
Over-absorbed overhead (W)			1,600
Absorption costing profit			48,400

Working:

		£
Overhead absorbed	(5,800 × £5)	29,000
Overhead incurred		27,400
Over-absorbed overhead		1,600

Task 13.5

(a) £ | 36.40

$$\frac{£582,400}{16,000} = £36.40$$

(b) £ | 33.00

$$\frac{£582,400 - £54,400}{16,000} = £33.00$$

(c) £ | 528,000

£33.00 × 16,000 units = £528,000 (or £582,400 − £54,400 = £528,000)

(d) £ | 454,400

£176,000 + £230,400 + £48,000 = £454,400

(e) £ | 28.40

$$\frac{£454,400}{16,000} = £28.40$$

Chapter 14

Task 14.1

(a) | 9,000 units | Breakeven point in units = Fixed costs/contribution per unit

$$= £45,000/(£22 - £17)$$

$$= 9,000 \text{ units}$$

(b) | £ | 198,000 | Breakeven point in units × selling price per unit

$$= 9,000 × £22$$

$$= £198,000$$

(c)

Units of COLIN sold	9,500	10,500
	£	£
Margin of safety (units)	500	1,500
Margin of safety percentage	$\left(\dfrac{500}{9,500} \times 100\%\right) =$ **5%**	$\left(\dfrac{1,500}{10,500} \times 100\%\right) =$ **14%**
Margin of safety revenue (units × sales price)	11,000	33,000

(d) | 13,000 units | Activity level $= \dfrac{\text{Fixed costs + target profit}}{\text{Contribution per unit}} = \dfrac{45,000 + 20,000}{5}$

$$= 13,000 \text{ units}$$

(e) The correct answer is: the breakeven point will decrease and the margin of safety will increase

••

Task 14.2

(a) $8,000 \times £(22 - 17) = £40,000$

(b) | £ | 132,000 | which is $(£30,000/£5 \times £22)$ or $(6,000 \times £22)$

(c)

Units of COLIN sold	6,500	7,000
	£	£
Margin of safety (units)	500	1,000
Margin of safety percentage	$\left(\dfrac{500}{6,500} \times 100\%\right) =$ **8%**	$\left(\dfrac{1,000}{7,000} \times 100\%\right) =$ **14%**

(d) | 8,000 units | Yes as it is at the maximum level of production.

....

Task 14.3

The correct answer is 3,000 units

$$\text{Breakeven point} = \frac{\text{Fixed costs}}{\text{Contribution per unit}} = \frac{£30,000}{£(15-5)} = 3,000 \text{ units}$$

If you selected 2,000 units you divided the fixed cost by the selling price, but remember that the selling price also has to cover the variable cost. 4,000 units is the margin of safety, and if you selected 6,000 units, you divided the fixed cost by the variable cost per unit.

....

Task 14.4

The correct answer is: 20%

$$\text{Breakeven point} = \frac{\text{Fixed costs}}{\text{Contribution per unit}} = \frac{£96,000}{£(12-8)} = 24,000 \text{ units}$$

Budgeted sales   <u>30,000</u> units

Margin of safety   <u>6,000</u> units

$$\text{Expressed as a \% of budget} = \frac{6,000}{30,000} \times 100\% = 20\%$$

If you selected 25% you calculated the correct margin of safety in units, but you then expressed this as a percentage of the breakeven point. If you selected 73% you divided the fixed cost by the selling price to determine the breakeven point, but the selling price also has to cover the variable cost. You should have been able to eliminate 125% as an option; the margin of safety expressed as a percentage must always be less than 100 per cent.

Task 14.5

(a) The correct answer is: 10,090 units

$$\text{Breakeven point} = \frac{\text{Fixed costs}}{\text{Contribution per unit}}$$

$$= \frac{10,000 \times £(4.00 + 0.80)}{(£6.00 - (£1.20 + £0.40))}$$

$$= \frac{£48,000}{£4.40} = 10,909 \text{ units}$$

If you selected 8,000 units you divided the fixed cost by the selling price, but the selling price also has to cover the variable cost. 8,333 units ignores the selling costs, but these are costs that must be covered before the breakeven point is reached. 10,000 units is the budgeted sales volume, which happens to be below the breakeven point.

(b) The correct answer is: 13,409 units

$$\text{Contribution required for target profit} = \text{fixed costs} + \text{profit}$$
$$= £48,000 + £11,000$$
$$= £59,000$$
$$\div \text{Contribution per unit (from part (a))} = £4.40$$
$$\therefore \text{Sales units required} = 13,409 \text{ units}$$

If you selected 2,500 units you divided the required profit by the contribution per unit, but the fixed costs must be covered before any profit can be earned. If you selected 9,833 units you identified correctly the contribution required for the target profit, but you then divided by the selling price per unit instead of the contribution per unit. 10,625 units ignores the selling costs, which must be covered before a profit can be earned.

Task 14.6

(a)

Forecast	Top4	Top5	Total
Contribution per unit (£) (W1)	6	9	
Contribution per kg (£) (W2)	16	18	
Ranking	2	1	
Total material available (kg)			1,125
Material allocated (kg)	375	750	
Number of units produced (W3)	1,000	1,500	
Total contribution earned (£) (W4)	6,000	13,500	19,500
Less: fixed costs (£)			10,000
Forecast profit/loss made (£)			9,500

Workings

W1: Top4 – £18,000/3,000 = £6
    Top5 – £13,500/1,500 = £9

W2: Top4 – £18,000/1,125 = £16
    Top5 – £13,500/750 = £18

W3: Top4 kg per unit = 1,125 kg/3,000 = 0.375 kg

∴ 375 kg/0.375 kg per unit = 1,000 units

W4: Top4 = 1,000 units × £6 = £6,000

Top5 = 1,500 units × £9 = £13,500

(b) Contract Top5 | should | be selected as the first contract to produce next month as it has the highest | contribution per kg used |.

Task 14.7

(a)

Forecast	Sun	Rain	Total
Contribution per unit (£) (W1)	3	4	
Contribution per hour (£) (W2)	4	2	
Ranking	1	2	
Total labour hours available (hours)			5,000
Labour hours allocated (hours)	2,250	2,750	
Number of units produced (W3)	3,000	1,375	
Total contribution earned (£) (W4)	9,000	5,500	14,500
Less: fixed costs (£)			7,000
Forecast profit/loss made (£)			7,500

Workings

W1: Sun – £9,000/3,000 = £3
      Rain – £6,000/1,500 = £4

W2: Sun – £9,000/2,250 = £4
      Rain – £6,000/3,000 = £2

W3: Rain hours per unit = 3,000/1,500 = 2 hours

      ∴2,750 hours/2 hours per unit = 1,375 units

W4: Sun = 3,000 units × £3 = £9,000

      Rain = 1,375 units × £4 = £5,500

Chapter 15

Task 15.1

(a) The net present value is **Negative**.

	Year 0 £000	Year 1 £000	Year 2 £000	Year 3 £000	Year 4 £000
Capital expenditure	(1,000)				
Sales income		350	400	400	350
Operating costs		(100)	(110)	(120)	(130)
Net cash flows	(1,000)	250	290	280	220
PV factors	1.0000	0.9009	0.8116	0.7312	0.6587
Discounted cash flows	(1,000)	225	235	205	145
Net present value	(190)				

(b) The payback period is **3** years and **10** months.

Task 15.2

£810,000. This is calculated as follows:

(all in £'000) 225 + 235 + 205 + 145 – capital expenditure = 0

Therefore capital expenditure = 810

Task 15.3

The net present value is **Positive**.

	Year 0 £000	Year 1 £000	Year 2 £000	Year 3 £000	Year 4 £000
Capital expenditure	(810)				
Sales income		350	400	400	350
Operating costs		(100)	(110)	(120)	(130)
Net cash flows	(810)	250	290	280	220
PV factors	1.0000	0.9346	0.8734	0.8163	0.7629
Discounted cash flows	(810)	234	253	229	168
Net present value	74				

Task 15.4

(a)

	Year 0 £	Year 1 £	Year 2 £	Year 3 £	Year 4 £
Net cash flows	−180,000	42,000	50,000	75,000	80,000
PV factors (15%)	1.000	0.8696	0.7561	0.6575	0.5718
Discounted cash flow	−180,000	36,523	37,805	49,313	45,744
NPV	−10,615				

(b)

	Year 0 £	Year 1 £	Year 2 £	Year 3 £	Year 4 £
Net cash flows	−180,000	42,000	50,000	75,000	80,000
PV factors (10%)	1.000	0.9090	0.8264	0.7513	0.6830
Discounted cash flow	−180,000	38,178	41,320	56,348	54,640
NPV	10,486				

(c) 12.5%

At a cost of capital of 15% the NPV is negative. At a cost of capital of 10% the NPV is positive. So an NPV of zero must be somewhere in between 10% and 15%.

Task 15.5

11.4%

The IRR is the cost of capital which gives an NPV of zero. As you can see from the table, the higher the cost of capital, the closer the NPV is getting to zero. Therefore 11.4% is the correct answer.

....

Task 15.6

IRR = 13.3%

$$IRR = A + \left[\frac{a}{a-b} \times (B - A) \right]$$

$$IRR = 12 + \left[\frac{6,000}{6,000 - -3,000} \times (14 - 12) \right]$$

$$IRR = 12 + \left[\frac{6,000}{6,000 + 3,000} \times 2 \right]$$

$$\therefore IRR = 12 + \left[\frac{6,000}{9,000} \times 2 \right]$$

$$\therefore IRR = 13.3\%$$

....

Task 15.7

Project B

The business is most interested in the return and therefore the decision should be based on the net present value. The project with the highest NPV gives the highest return and therefore Project B should be chosen.

....

Task 15.8

Project A

The business is most interested in limiting risk and therefore the decision should be based on the payback period. The project with the quickest payback gives the lowest risk and therefore Project A should be chosen.

....

Task 15.9

Statement	True	False
If the cost of capital is greater than the IRR for a project, then the project is worthwhile.		✓
The IRR is the discount rate which gives a zero NPV.	✓	
The payback method uses cash flows from a project to determine the payback period.	✓	
The shorter the payback period of a project, the lower the risk.	✓	

AAT AQ2016 SAMPLE ASSESSMENT 1 MANAGEMENT ACCOUNTING: COSTING

Time allowed: 2 hours and 30 minutes

Management Accounting: Costing (MMAC)
AAT sample assessment 1

Task 1 (16 marks)

Crest Paints Ltd had the following containers of red pigment in inventory:

Date purchased	Quantity	Cost per container £	Total cost £
November 28	280	16.0	4,480
December 4	320	16.5	5,280
December 10	160	16.9	2,704

Drag and drop the correct cost into the cost column of the table below to record issuing 350 of these containers on 11 December and to record the inventory balance after the issue using:

- **AVCO (weighted average cost)**
- **FIFO (first in, first out)**

	Cost
AVCO issue	
FIFO issue	
AVCO balance	
FIFO balance	

£5,635	£6,670
£5,740	£6,690
£5,839	£6,724
£6,625	£6,829

Task 2 (16 marks)

Below are extracts from Crest Paints Ltd's payroll for last week.

Date	Labour costs
8 December	Paint manufacture: Production employees' pay 590 hours at £10 per hour
10 December	Canning and packing: Production employees' basic pay £5,600 + £500 overtime
12 December	Stores department: Employees' pay £2,000 + 15% bonus
14 December	General Administration department: Staff salaries £4,000 + 20% bonus

Complete the cost journal entries to record the four payroll payments made last week.

Date	Code	Debit £	Credit £
8 December	▼		
8 December	▼		
10 December	▼		
10 December	▼		
12 December	▼		
12 December	▼		
14 December	▼		
14 December	▼		

Drop-down list

6001 Paint manufacture direct costs
6002 Canning and packing direct costs
7000 Operating overheads
8000 Non-operating overheads
5000 Wages control account

Task 3 (12 marks)

Employees work in teams, of five employees each, in the packing section of Crest Paints Ltd (CPL). They are paid a basic rate of £12.00 per hour, and any overtime is paid at the following rates:

- Overtime rate 1 – basic pay + 50%
- Overtime rate 2 – double the rate of basic rate

CPL sets a target for packing boxes of paint each month. A bonus equal to 25% of the basic hourly rate is payable for every box packed in the month in excess of the target.

The target for December for Team 3 was 2,475 boxes, however, the team actually packed 2,775 boxes.

All team members work the same number of hours.
All overtime and bonuses are included as part of the direct labour cost.

(a) **Complete the gaps in the table below to calculate the total labour cost for Team 3.**

Labour cost	Hours	£
Basic pay	700	
Overtime rate 1	60	
Overtime rate 2	30	
Total cost before bonus	790	
Bonus payment		
Total cost including bonus		

(b) **Calculate the total labour cost of packing each box in the month of December.**

The total labour cost of packing each box in the month of December is:

£ [   ] .

There are five employees in Team 3.

(c) Complete the following sentence.

The basic pay and overtime for each member of Team 3 for December was:

£ [   ]   and the bonus payable to each team member was:

£ [   ] .

....

Task 4 (18 marks)

Crest Paints Ltd calculates depreciation on a reducing balance basis, and allocates/apportions other overheads using the most appropriate basis for each.

(a) Complete the table below to identify a suitable basis for allocating or apportioning each overhead by selecting the most appropriate option from the picklist.

Overhead	Basis of apportionment
Depreciation of mixing equipment	▼
Rent and rates of production departments	▼
Quality control costs	▼
Canning equipment maintenance costs	▼
Canning equipment insurance costs	▼

Drop-down list

Age of mixing equipment
Carrying value of mixing equipment
Carrying value on canning equipment
Factory floor space
Head office floor space
Number of maintenance employees
Number of quality control inspections
Replacement cost of mixing equipment
Time spent servicing canning equipment

Crest Paints Ltd has already allocated and apportioned its current overhead costs for the next quarter, as shown in the table below. These costs have yet to be reapportioned to the two profit centres of Paint Manufacture and Canning & Packing.

The General Administration department services the two profit centres, the Maintenance department and the Stores department. These costs are to be reapportioned 40% to the Paint Manufacture profit centre; 40% to the Canning & Packing profit centre; and 10% each to the Maintenance and Stores departments.

The Stores costs are reapportioned on the basis of inventory requisitions. The Paint Manufacture profit centre expects to have 8,280 requisitions and the Canning & Packing profit centre expects to have 5,520 requisitions.

The Maintenance department reapportions costs on the basis of maintenance hours. The Paint Manufacture profit centre expects to use 7,000 maintenance hours and the Canning & Packing profit centre expects to use 5,500 maintenance hours.

(b) Complete the table by reapportioning costs on the basis of the information given above. Enter your answers in whole pounds only. Indicate negative figures with minus signs, NOT brackets.

Each cell in the bottom five rows must have an entry in order to gain full marks.

	Paint Manufacture £	Canning & Packing £	Maintenance £	Stores £	General Admin £	Totals £
Depreciation of equipment	634,000	815,000	115,000	87,000	167,000	1,818,000
Heat and light of premises	178,000	197,000	26,000	32,000	43,000	476,000
Rent and rates of premises	273,000	311,000	64,000	96,000	82,000	826,000
Administration costs					185,000	185,000
Indirect labour costs	146,000	138,000	151,000	121,000	197,000	753,000
Totals	1,231,000	1,461,000	356,000	336,000	674,000	4,058,000
Reapportion General Administration						
Reapportion Stores						
Reapportion Maintenance						
Total overheads to profit centres						4,058,000

Another overhead is machine running costs. The estimated cost for the next quarter is £630,000 which consists of a fixed element and a variable element. The fixed element is 60% of the total cost and the rest is variable. The fixed element of the total cost is to be apportioned between the Paint Manufacture profit centre and the Canning & Packing profit centre in the ratio 56:44. The variable element of the total cost is apportioned in the ratio of 62:38.

(c) **Complete the following sentences by inserting the correct values.**

The fixed element of the machine running costs that will be apportioned to the Paint Manufacture profit centre is:

£

The variable element of the machine running cost that will be apportioned to the Canning & Packing profit centre is:

£

Task 5 (15 marks)

Crest Paints Ltd has the following information about its two profit centres:

Quarter 1	Paint Manufacture	Canning & Packing
Budgeted direct labour hours	7,032	8,864
Budgeted machine hours	2,966	2,220
Actual direct labour hours	6,815	8,000
Actual machine hours	3,217	2,312
Budgeted overheads	£185,375	£223,060
Actual overheads	£179,425	£215,404

(a) **Calculate the budgeted overhead absorption rate for the Paint Manufacture profit centre based on machine hours, and that for the Canning & Packing profit centre based on direct labour hours. Show your answers to TWO decimal places.**

	Paint Manufacture £	Canning & Packing £
Budgeted overhead absorption rate	☐ per hour	☐ per hour

Now suppose for Quarter 2 that the overhead absorption rate for the Paint Manufacture profit centre had been based on direct labour hours, and was £28 per hour. The actual overheads were £213,200 and the actual labour hours worked were 7,400 hours.

(b) **Complete the following table.**

	Overheads incurred £	Overheads absorbed £	Difference absorbed £	Under/over absorption £
Paint Manufacture profit centre				▼

Drop-down list

over
under

(c) **Refer to the information for Quarter 1, at the start of the task, and complete the following sentence.**

In Quarter 1 overheads for the Canning & Packing profit centre were

☐ ▼   by   £ ☐ .

Drop-down list

over-absorbed
under-absorbed

Task 6 (25 marks)

Crest Paints Ltd (CPL) is planning to launch a new water resistant emulsion paint for bathrooms and kitchens called WR52. This will be manufactured in batches of 50,000 cans.

The following cost estimates have been produced per batch of WR52.

Paint WR52 cost estimates	£
Direct material per batch	103,000
Direct labour per batch	105,000
Variable production overheads per batch	84,000
Fixed production overheads per batch	34,000
Administration, selling and distribution costs per batch	41,000
Total costs	367,000

(a) **Calculate the estimated prime cost per BATCH of WR52.**

£

(b) **Calculate the estimated marginal production cost per BATCH of WR52.**

£

(c) **Calculate the estimated full absorption cost of one BATCH of WR52.**

£

(d) **Calculate the estimated marginal production cost of one CAN of WR52 (round to TWO decimal places).**

£

(e) **Calculate the estimated full absorption cost of one CAN of WR52 (round to TWO decimal places).**

£

(f) **Which of the following costs would NEVER be included in CPL's inventory valuation?**

	✓
Marginal costs	
Period costs	
Prime costs	
Product costs	

(g) **Which of these is an example of unethical behaviour by one of CPL's accounting technicians?**

	✓
Calculating profits objectively rather than subjectively	
Valuing inventory so as to maximise a period's profits	
Treating CPL's costs as confidential	
Allocating CPL's costs between products objectively	

(h) **Why might CPL decide to allocate its costs between the products of different departments?**

	✓
To comply with accounting standards	
To reduce its overall inventory valuation	
To report segmented profits/losses	
To speed up its internal reporting	

CPL's Paint Manufacturing Department is a profit centre.

(i) **Which of the following does its management control?**

	✓
The department's variable costs	
To department's total (variable and fixed) costs	
The department's total costs and revenues	
The department's total costs, revenues, assets and liabilities	

Task 7 (16 marks)

(a) **Choose the correct description for each of the three terms below.**

Term	Description	
Contribution		▼
Breakeven revenue		▼
Margin of safety		▼

Drop-down list

Excess of actual sales over breakeven sales
Excess of breakeven sales over actual sales
Planned revenue less costs
Point where selling price equals variable costs
Profit level before fixed costs
Sales revenue where there is neither profit nor loss
Sales volume where there is neither profit nor loss
Selling price less total costs
Selling price less variable costs
Selling price plus variable costs

Crest Paints Ltd (CPL) manufactures MP16, a marine paint for boats. MP16 is made in batches of 10,000 cans, each of which is sold for £5.00. The following are the costs involved in its manufacture:

Batch of 10,000 units of MP16	£
Direct material	4,810
Direct labour	7,508
Variable overheads	7,682
Fixed overheads	57,000

(b) **Calculate the breakeven volume of MP16.**

[   ] cans

(c) **Calculate the breakeven sales revenue of MP16.**

£ [   ]

CPL also manufactures and sells another marine paint, MP17. This is manufactured in batches of 12,000 cans and makes a contribution of £42,000 per batch. Fixed costs of production are £56,000. CPL has set a target profit of £31,500 from manufacturing and selling this paint.

(d) **Calculate the margin of safety of MP17 (in cans) if CPL sells 20,000 cans.**

☐ cans

(e) **How many cans of MP17 must CPL sell to reach its target profit of £31,500?**

☐ cans

Task 8 (16 marks)

The following eight options describe the behaviour of different types of costs during a short period of one quarter of a year.

Option	Description
1	Increases in total as volume increases
2	Decreases in total as volume increases
3	Increases per unit as selling price increases
4	Decreases per unit as selling price increases

Option	Description
5	Decreases per unit as volume increases
6	Made up of fixed and variable costs
7	Fixed for a certain volume range only
8	Variable for a certain volume range only

Drag and drop the correct option into the box below to show the correct description for the following four types of cost.

	Description
Fixed cost	
Variable cost	
Semi-variable cost	
Stepped cost	

Option 1	Option 5
Option 2	Option 6
Option 3	Option 7
Option 4	Option 8

Task 9 (16 marks)

Crest Paints Ltd (CPL) had budgeted to manufacture and sell 50,000 cans of gloss paint GL78 in December. However, due to a shortage of solvent, it was only able to manufacture and sell 45,000 cans. CPL's manufacturing costs are all variable except for fixed overheads.

(a) **Complete the following table to show a flexed budget and the resulting variances against the budget for GL78 in December. Show the actual variance amount for sales revenue and each cost in the column headed 'Variance'.**

Note:

- **Adverse variances must be denoted with a minus sign or brackets.**

- **Enter 0 where any figure is zero.**

	Original budget	Flexed budget	Actual	Variance
Number of cans	50,000	45,000	45,000	
	£	£	£	£
Sales revenue	225,000		207,400	
Less costs:				
Direct materials and direct labour	45,200		46,160	
Variable overheads	36,400		31,610	
Fixed overheads	74,800		75,300	
Profit from operations	68,600		54,330	

(b) **Referring to your answer for part (a), which one of the variances has had the greatest impact in increasing the profit from operations?**

	✓
Sales revenue	
Direct materials and direct labour	
Variable overheads	
Fixed overheads	

(c) **Which one of the following might have caused the variance for direct materials and direct labour costs?**

	✓
A decrease in material prices	
A decrease in employees' pay	
An increase in material prices	
More efficient usage of direct labour	

Task 10 (20 marks)

Crest Paints Ltd is considering a possible capital investment project. It will base its decision upon using three appraisal methods, the results of which are shown below:

Appraisal method	Notes	Company policy	Project results
Payback period		2.5 years	3 years
Net Present Value (NPV)	Discount at 15% cost of capital	Accept if positive	£50,000 +ve
Internal Rate of Return (IRR)	Discount at 15% cost of capital	Must exceed cost of capital	14%

Identify the correct recommendation for each decision below by dragging the appropriate option into the table.

Appraisal method	Recommendation
Payback	
NPV	
IRR	
Overall	

Options:

Accept as positive	Reject as per most important investment criterion
Reject as more than 2.5 years	Accept as greater than cost of capital
Reject as positive	Reject as less than cost of capital
Accept as more than 2.5 years	Accept as per most important investment criterion

AAT AQ2016 SAMPLE ASSESSMENT 1
MANAGEMENT ACCOUNTING:
COSTING

ANSWERS

Management Accounting: Costing (MMAC)
AAT sample assessment 1

Task 1 (16 marks)

Drag and drop the correct cost into the cost column of the table to record issuing 350 of these containers on 11 December and to record the inventory balance after the issue using:

- **AVCO (weighted average cost)**
- **FIFO (first in, first out)**

	Cost £
AVCO issue	5,740
FIFO issue	5,635
AVCO balance	6,724
FIFO balance	6,829

£6,670

£6,690

£5,839

£6,625

Task 2 (16 marks)

Complete the cost journal entries to record the four payroll payments made last week.

Date	Code	Debit £	Credit £
8 December	6001 Paint manufacture direct costs	5,900	
8 December	5000 Wages control account		5,900
10 December	6002 Canning and packing direct costs	6,100	
10 December	5000 Wages control account		6,100
12 December	7000 Operating overheads	2,300	
12 December	5000 Wages control account		2,300
14 December	8000 Non-operating overheads	4,800	
14 December	5000 Wages control account		4,800

Task 3 (12 marks)

(a) **Complete the gaps in the table below to calculate the total labour cost for Team 3.**

Labour cost	Hours	£
Basic pay	700	8,400
Overtime rate 1	60	1,080
Overtime rate 2	30	720
Total cost before bonus	790	10,200
Bonus payment		900
Total cost including bonus		11,100

(b) **Calculate the total labour cost of packing each box in the month of December.**

The total labour cost of packing each box in the month of December is:

£ 4 .

(c) Complete the following sentence.

The basic pay and overtime for each member of Team 3 for December was:

| £ | 2,040 |

and the bonus payable to each team member was:

| £ | 180 |

.

....

Task 4 (18 marks)

(a) Complete the table below to identify a suitable basis for allocating or apportioning each overhead by selecting the most appropriate option from the picklist.

Overhead	Basis of apportionment
Depreciation of mixing equipment	Carrying value of mixing equipment
Rent and rates of production departments	Factory floor space
Quality control costs	Number of quality control inspections
Canning equipment maintenance costs	Time spent servicing canning equipment
Canning equipment insurance costs	Carrying value of canning equipment

(b) Complete the table by reapportioning costs on the basis of the information given above. Enter your answers in whole pounds only. Indicate negative figures with minus signs, NOT brackets.

	Paint Manufacture £	Canning & Packing £	Maintenance £	Stores £	General Admin £	Totals £
Depreciation of equipment	634,000	815,000	115,000	87,000	167,000	1,818,000
Heat and light of premises	178,000	197,000	26,000	32,000	43,000	476,000
Rent and rates of premises	273,000	311,000	64,000	96,000	82,000	826,000
Administration costs					185,000	185,000
Indirect labour costs	146,000	138,000	151,000	121,000	197,000	753,000
Totals	1,231,000	1,461,000	356,000	336,000	674,000	4,058,000
Reapportion General Administration	269,600	269,600	67,400	67,400	-674,000	
Reapportion Stores	242,040	161,360		-403,400		
Reapportion Maintenance	237,104	186,296	-423,400			
Total overheads to profit centres	1,979,744	2,078,256				4,058,000

(c) Complete the following sentences by inserting the correct values.

The fixed element of the machine running costs that will be apportioned to the Paint Manufacture profit centre is:

£	211,680

The variable element of the machine running cost that will be apportioned to the Canning & Packing profit centre is:

£	95,760

Task 5 (15 marks)

(a) **Calculate the budgeted overhead absorption rate for the Paint Manufacture profit centre based on machine hours, and that for the Canning & Packing profit centre based on direct labour hours. Show your answers to TWO decimal places.**

	Paint Manufacture £	Canning & Packing £
Budgeted overhead absorption rate	62.50 per hour	25.16 per hour

(b) **Complete the following table.**

	Overheads incurred £	Overheads absorbed £	Difference absorbed £	Under/over absorption
Paint Manufacture profit centre	213,200	207,200	6,000	under

(c) **Refer to the information for Quarter 1, at the start of the task, and complete the following sentence.**

In Quarter 1 overheads for the Canning & Packing profit centre were

| under-absorbed | by | £ | 14,124 | .

....

Task 6 (25 marks)

(a) **Calculate the estimated prime cost per BATCH of WR52.**

| £ | 208,000 |

(b) **Calculate the estimated marginal production cost per BATCH of WR52.**

| £ | 292,000 |

(c) **Calculate the estimated full absorption cost of one BATCH of WR52.**

£	326,000

(d) **Calculate the estimated marginal production cost of one CAN of WR52 (round to TWO decimal places).**

£	5.84

(e) **Calculate the estimated full absorption cost of one CAN of WR52 (round to TWO decimal places).**

£	6.52

(f) **Which of the following costs would NEVER be included in CPL's inventory valuation?**

	✓
Marginal costs	
Period costs	✓
Prime costs	
Product costs	

(g) **Which of these is an example of unethical behaviour by one of CPL's accounting technicians?**

	✓
Calculating profits objectively rather than subjectively	
Valuing inventory so as to maximise a period's profits	✓
Treating CPL's costs as confidential	
Allocating CPL's costs between products objectively	

(h) **Why might CPL decide to allocate its costs between the products of different departments?**

	✓
To comply with accounting standards	
To reduce its overall inventory valuation	
To report segmented profits/losses	✓
To speed up its internal reporting	

CPL's Paint Manufacturing Department is a profit centre.

(i) **Which of the following does its management control?**

	✓
The department's variable costs	
To department's total (variable and fixed) costs	
The department's total costs and revenues	✓
The department's total costs, revenues, assets and liabilities	

Task 7 (16 marks)

(a) **Choose the correct description for each of the three terms below.**

Term	Description
Contribution	Selling price less variable costs
Breakeven revenue	Sales revenue where there is neither profit nor loss
Margin of safety	Excess of actual sales over breakeven sales

(b) **Calculate the breakeven volume of MP16.**

  19,000 cans

(c) **Calculate the breakeven sales revenue of MP16.**

  £ 95,000

(d) **Calculate the margin of safety of MP17 (in cans) if CPL sells 20,000 cans.**

  4,000 cans

(e) **How many cans of MP17 must CPL sell to reach its target profit of £31,500?**

  25,000 cans

Task 8 (16 marks)

Drag and drop the correct option into the box below to show the correct description for the following four types of cost.

	Description
Fixed cost	Option 5
Variable cost	Option 1
Semi-variable cost	Option 6
Stepped cost	Option 7

Option 2

Option 3

Option 4   Option 8

Task 9 (16 marks)

(a)   Complete the following table to show a flexed budget and the resulting variances against the budget for GL78 in December. Show the actual variance amount for sales revenue and each cost in the column headed 'Variance'.

Note:

- Adverse variances must be denoted with a minus sign or brackets.

- Enter 0 where any figure is zero.

	Original budget	Flexed budget	Actual	Variance
Number of cans	50,000	45,000	45,000	
	£	£	£	£
Sales revenue	225,000	202,500	207,400	4,900
Less costs:				
Direct materials and direct labour	45,200	40,680	46,160	–5,480
Variable overheads	36,400	32,760	31,610	1,150
Fixed overheads	74,800	74,800	75,300	–500
Profit from operations	68,600	54,260	54,330	

(b) **Referring to your answer for part (a), which one of the variances has had the greatest impact in increasing the profit from operations?**

	✓
Sales revenue	✓
Direct materials and direct labour	
Variable overheads	
Fixed overheads	

(c) **Which one of the following might have caused the variance for direct materials and direct labour costs?**

	✓
A decrease in material prices	
A decrease in employees' pay	
An increase in material prices	✓
More efficient usage of direct labour	

Task 10 (20 marks)

Identify the correct recommendation for each decision below by dragging the appropriate option into the table.

Appraisal method	Recommendation
Payback	Reject as more than 2.5 years
NPV	Accept as positive
IRR	Reject as less than cost of capital
Overall	Accept as per most important investment criterion

Options:

Reject as per most important investment criterion

Accept as greater than cost of capital

Reject as positive

Accept as more than 2.5 years

AAT AQ2016 SAMPLE ASSESSMENT 2 MANAGEMENT ACCOUNTING: COSTING

Time allowed: 2 hours and 30 minutes

You are advised to attempt sample assessment 2 online from the AAT website. This will ensure you are prepared for how assessments will be presented on the AAT's system when you attempt the real assessment.

https://www.aat.org.uk/training/study-support/search

BPP PRACTICE ASSESSMENT 1 MANAGEMENT ACCOUNTING: COSTING

Time allowed: 2 hours and 30 minutes

BPP
LEARNING MEDIA

Management Accounting: Costing (MMAC)
BPP practice assessment 1

Task 1

Claridges Ltd had the following kg of fibreglass panels in inventory:

Date purchased	Quantity kg	Cost per kg £	Total cost £
June 29	750	2.30	1,725
July 6	500	2.00	1,000
July 21	250	2.60	650

Drag and drop the correct cost into the cost column of the table below to record issuing 400 kg on 22 July and to record the inventory balance after the issue using:

- **AVCO (weighted average cost)**
- **LIFO (last in, first out)**

	Cost £
AVCO issue	
LIFO issue	
AVCO balance	
LIFO balance	

£900	£2,425
£920	£2,455
£950	£2,475
£1,500	£3,375

Task 2

Below are extracts from Claridges Ltd's payroll for July.

Date	Labour costs
1 July	Production employees' basic wages cost of 610 hours at £15 per hour
8 July	Indirect production salaries of £3,000 + 12% bonus
10 July	Admin department salaries of £3,500 + 15% bonus
14 July	Production employees' overtime requested by the customer of 30 hours at £15 per hour

Complete the cost journal entries to record the four payroll payments made last week.

Picklist:

Direct labour cost
Non-production overheads
Production overheads
Wages control account

Date	Entry	Debit £	Credit £
1 July	▼		
1 July	▼		
8 July	▼		
8 July	▼		
10 July	▼		
10 July	▼		

Date	Entry		Dr £	Cr £
14 July		▼		
14 July		▼		

Task 3

At Claridges Ltd, employees work in teams of three employees, in department A. They are paid a basic rate of £20.00 per hour, and any overtime is paid at the following rates:

- Overtime rate 1 – basic pay + 50%
- Overtime rate 2 – double the rate of basic rate

Claridges sets a target for number of units produced each month. A bonus equal to 30% of the basic hourly rate is payable for every unit in the month in excess of the target.

The target for July for department A was 400 units, however, the department actually produced 450 units.

All team members work the same number of hours.
All overtime and bonuses are included as part of the direct labour cost.

(a) Complete the gaps in the table below to calculate the total labour cost for department A.

Labour cost	Hours	£
Basic pay	300	
Overtime rate 1	20	
Overtime rate 2	30	
Total cost before bonus	350	
Bonus payment		
Total cost including bonus		

(b) **Calculate the total labour cost of producing each unit in the month of July.**

The total labour cost of producing each unit in the month of July is:

£ [   ] .

There are three employees in department A.

(c) **Complete the following sentence.**

The basic pay and overtime for each member of department A for July was:

£ [   ]   and the bonus payable to each team member was:

£ [   ] .

....

Task 4

Claridges Ltd apportions overheads using the most appropriate basis.

(a) **Complete the table below to identify a suitable basis for allocating or apportioning each overhead by selecting the most appropriate option from the picklist.**

Overhead	Basis of apportionment	
Depreciation of equipment		▼
Power for production machinery		▼
Rent and rates for admin department		▼
Equipment insurance		▼
Canteen costs		▼

Picklist:

Factory floor space
Head office floor space
NBV of equipment
Number of employees
Number of orders executed
Number of production runs
Production machinery power usage (KwH)

(b) Claridges Ltd has already allocated and apportioned its current overhead costs for the next period as shown in the table below. These costs have yet to be apportioned to the two profit centres of Glass moulding and Glass extrusion.

- 45% of the Maintenance cost centre's time is spent maintaining production machinery in the Glass moulding production centre, and the remainder in the Glass extrusion production centre.

- The Stores cost centre makes 35% of its issues to the Glass moulding production centre, and 65% to the Glass extrusion production centre.

- General Administration supports the two production centres equally.

- There is no reciprocal servicing between the three support cost centres.

Complete the table showing the reapportionment of overheads to the two production centres. Enter your answers in whole pounds only. Indicate negative figures with minus signs, NOT brackets.

	Basis of apportionment	Glass moulding £	Glass extrusion £	Maintenance £	Stores £	General Admin £	Totals £
Depreciation of plant and equipment	NBV of plant and equipment	312,708	437,792				750,500
Power for production machinery	Production machinery power usage (KwH)	1,028,963	846,037				1,875,000
Rent and rates	Floor space			40,167	48,200	32,133	120,500
Light and heat	Floor space			10,833	13,000	8,667	32,500
Indirect labour	Allocated			115,000	37,850	225,000	377,850
Totals		1,341,671	1,283,829	166,000	99,050	265,800	3,156,350
Reapportion Maintenance							
Reapportion Stores							

	Basis of apportionment	Glass moulding £	Glass extrusion £	Maintenance £	Stores £	General Admin £	Totals £
Reapportion General Admin							
Total overheads to production centres							

(c) Another overhead is estimated to be £570,000 for the period. It consists of a fixed element and a variable element. The fixed element is 30% of the total cost and the rest is variable. The fixed element of the total cost is to be apportioned between the glass moulding and glass intrusion centres in the ratio 65:35. The variable element of the total cost is apportioned in the ratio 46:54.

Complete the following sentences by inserting the correct values.

The fixed element that will be apportioned to the glass extrusion profit centre is:

£ [   ]

The variable element that will be apportioned to the glass moulding profit centre is:

£ [   ]

Task 5

Claridges Ltd has the following information about its two profit centres:

Quarter 1	Metal bashing	Metal extrusion
Budgeted direct labour hours	42,750	24,750
Budgeted machine hours	13,145	8,250
Actual direct labour hours	43,100	22,275
Actual machine hours	12,936	8,975
Budgeted overheads	£814,990	£445,500
Actual overheads	£789,765	£495,250

(a) **Calculate the budgeted overhead absorption rate for the Metal bashing profit centre based on machine hours, and that for the Metal extrusion profit centre based on direct labour hours. Show your answers to TWO decimal places.**

	Metal bashing £	Metal extrusion £
Budgeted overhead absorption rate	☐ per hour	☐ per hour

Now suppose for Quarter 2 that the overhead absorption rate for the Metal extrusion profit centre had been based on direct machine hours, and was £55 per hour. The actual overheads were £462,500 and the actual machine hours were 8,500 hours.

(b) **Complete the following table.**

	Overheads incurred £	Overheads absorbed £	Difference absorbed £	Under/over absorption £
Metal extrusion profit centre				▼

Picklist:

over
under

(c) **Refer to the information for Quarter 1, at the start of the task, and complete the following sentence.**

In Quarter 1 overheads for the Metal bashing profit centre were

☐ ▼ by £ ☐ .

Picklist:

over-absorbed
under-absorbed

Task 6

The Metal extrusion department of Claridges Ltd uses batch costing for some of its products.

The product DD1 is made in one batch of 62,000 units and the budgeted costs are as follows.

Description	Cost per batch £
Direct material	77,500
Direct labour	83,700
Variable overheads	12,400
Fixed manufacturing overheads	31,000
Fixed administration, selling and distribution costs	18,600
Total costs	223,200

(a) **Calculate the total cost of one unit of DD1.**

The total cost of one unit of DD1 is £ [   ]

(b) **Calculate the full absorption cost of one unit of DD1.**

The full absorption cost of one unit of DD1 is £ [   ]

(c) **Calculate the marginal cost of one unit of DD1.**

The marginal cost of one unit of DD1 is £ [   ]

(d) **Calculate the marginal production cost of one batch of DD1.**

The marginal production cost of one batch of DD1 is £ [   ]

(e) **Calculate the full absorption cost of one batch of DD1.**

The full absorption cost of one batch of DD1 is £ [   ]

(f) **Which of the following means the total direct costs?**

	✓
Production cost	
Variable cost	
Overhead cost	
Prime cost	

(g) **Which of the following principles means being straightforward and honest?**

	✓
Objectivity	
Integrity	
Confidentiality	
Competence	

(h) **Which of the following shows how particular sections of the business generate sales, costs and profits?**

	✓
Segmented report	
Financial report	
Overhead report	
Inventory report	

(i) **Claridges Ltd has a department which is an investment centre. Which of the following does its management control?**

	✓
The department's variable costs only	
The department's total (variable and fixed) costs only	
The department's total costs and revenues	
The department's total costs, revenues, assets and liabilities	

Task 7

(a) **Choose the correct description for each of the three terms below.**

Term	Description	
Limiting factor		▼
Breakeven point		▼
Target profit		▼

Picklist:

(Contribution per unit x target activity level) less fixed costs
Circumstance hindering quantity of units a business may make or sell
Excess of actual sales over breakeven sales
Excess of breakeven sales over actual sales
Planned revenue less costs
Point where selling price equals variable costs
Profit level before fixed costs
Sales revenue where there is neither profit nor loss
Sales volume where there is neither profit nor loss
Selling price less variable costs
Selling price plus variable costs

Claridges Ltd manufactures the alphapop, which has a selling price of £20 per unit, and a total variable cost of £12 per unit. Claridges Ltd estimates that the fixed costs per quarter associated with this product are £46,000.

(b) **Calculate the budgeted breakeven, in units, for the alphapop.**

	units

(c) **Calculate the budgeted breakeven, in £s, for the alphapop.**

£	

(d) **Calculate the margin of safety (in units) if Claridges sells 6,000 units of alphapop.**

	units

(e) **If Claridges Ltd wishes to make a profit of £20,000, how many units of the alphapop must it sell?**

	units

Task 8

The following eight options are costs incurred by Claridges Ltd during the quarter.

Select the correct cost behaviour option for each cost.

	Fixed cost	Variable cost	Semi-variable cost	Stepped cost
Material cost of £3 per unit				
Rent cost of £300				
Labour cost of £10 per unit				
Telephone bill of £20 per quarter plus £0.50 per phone call				
Supervisor cost of £5,000				
Insurance cost of £150				
Machine leasing cost £500 per 4,000 units				
Machinery depreciation of £100 based on machine hours used				

Task 9

Claridges Ltd budgeted to sell 250,000 units of the BEPPO for the year ending 31 July. However, actual sales volume was 360,000 units.

(a) **Complete the table below to show a flexed budget and the resulting variances against the budget for the Beppo in July. Show the actual variance amount for sales revenue and each cost in the column headed 'Variance'.**

Note:

- **Adverse variances must be denoted with a minus sign or brackets.**

- **Enter 0 where any figure is zero.**

	Original budget	Flexed budget	Actual	Variance
Volume sold	250,000	360,000	360,000	
	£000	£000	£000	£000
Sales revenue	5,000		9,000	
Less costs:				
Direct materials	875		1,325	
Direct labour	1,000		1,200	
Overheads	2,450		3,070	
Profit from operations	675		3,405	

(b) **Referring to your answer for part (a), which one of the variances has had the greatest impact in increasing the profit from operations?**

	✓
Sales revenue	
Direct materials	
Direct labour	
Overheads	

(c) **Which one of the following might have caused the variance for direct labour costs?**

	✓
A decrease in material prices	
An increase in employees' pay	
An increase in material prices	
More efficient usage of direct labour	

Task 10

Claridges Ltd is considering a possible capital investment project. It will base its decision upon using three appraisal methods. Each method has advantages and disadvantages

(a) **Complete the table below by dragging the appropriate option into the table.**

Appraisal method	Feature
Payback	
NPV	
IRR	
	Most important investment criterion

Options:

Ignores the time value of money	Discount rate that gives a NPV of zero
Payback	Accept project if appraisal method gives a positive figure
IRR	NPV

Estimates have been made for the initial capital cost, sales income and operating costs of the replacement machine, which is expected to have a useful life of three years:

	Year 0 £000	Year 1 £000	Year 2 £000	Year 3 £000
Capital expenditure	2,250			
Net cash inflows:		750	1,025	1,525

(b) Calculate the payback period of the proposed replacement machine to the nearest whole month.

The payback period is [   ] year(s) and [   ] month(s).

··

BPP PRACTICE ASSESSMENT 1
MANAGEMENT ACCOUNTING: COSTING

ANSWERS

Management Accounting: Costing (MMAC)
BPP practice assessment 1

Task 1

	Cost £
AVCO issue	900
LIFO issue	950
AVCO balance	2,475
LIFO balance	2,425

£920		£2,455

£1,500		£3,375

Workings:

AVCO cost per kg = (£1,725 + £1,000 + £650)/(750 + 500 + 250) = £2.25

AVCO issue cost of 400 kg = £2.25 × 400 = £900

AVCO closing balance = (1,500 – 400) × £2.25 = £2,475

LIFO issue cost of 400 kg = (250 kg × £2.60) + (150 kg × £2.00) = £950

LIFO closing balance = (350 kg × £2.00) + £1,725 = £2,425

Task 2

Date	Entry	Debit £	Credit £
1 July	Direct labour cost	9,150	
1 July	Wages control account		9,150
8 July	Production overheads	3,360	
8 July	Wages control account		3,360
10 July	Non-production overheads	4,025	
10 July	Wages control account		4,025

Date	Entry	Debit £	Credit £
14 July	Direct labour cost	450	
14 July	Wages control account		450

Task 3

(a)

Labour cost	Hours	Working	£
Basic pay	300	× £20.00	6,000
Overtime rate 1	20	× £20.00 × 1.5	600
Overtime rate 2	30	× £20.00 × 2	1,200
Total cost before bonus	350		7,800
Bonus payment		(450 – 400) × £20.00 × 30%	300
Total cost including bonus			8,100

(b) The total labour cost of producing each unit in the month of July is:

£	18

£8,100/450 = £18

(c) The basic pay and overtime for each member of department A for July was:

£	2,600

and the bonus payable to each team member was:

£	100

£7,800/3 = £2,600

£300/3 = £100

BPP
LEARNING MEDIA

Task 4

(a)

Overhead	Basis of apportionment
Depreciation of equipment	NBV of equipment
Power for production machinery	Production machinery power usage (KwH)
Rent and rates for admin department	Head office floor space
Equipment insurance	NBV of equipment
Canteen costs	Number of employees

(b)

	Basis of apportionment	Glass moulding £	Glass extrusion £	Maintenance £	Stores £	General Admin £	Totals £
Depreciation of plant and equipment	NBV of plant and equipment	312,708	437,792				750,500
Power for production machinery	Production machinery power usage (KwH)	1,028,963	846,037				1,875,000
Rent and rates	Floor space			40,167	48,200	32,133	120,500
Light and heat	Floor space			10,833	13,000	8,667	32,500
Indirect labour	Allocated			115,000	37,850	225,000	377,850
Totals		1,341,671	1,283,829	166,000	99,050	265,800	3,156,350
Reapportion Maintenance		74,700	91,300	−166,000			
Reapportion Stores		34,668	64,382		−99,050		
Reapportion General Admin		132,900	132,900			−265,800	
Total overheads to production centres		1,583,939	1,572,411				3,156,350

(c) The fixed element that will be apportioned to the glass extrusion profit centre is:

£	59,850

Fixed element = £570,000 × 30% = £171,000

Fixed element for glass extrusion = £171,000 × (35/100) = £59,850

The variable element that will be apportioned to the glass moulding profit centre is:

£	183,540

Variable element = £570,000 × 70% = £399,000

Variable element for glass moulding = £399,000 × (46/100) = £183,540

Task 5

(a)

	Metal bashing £	Metal extrusion £
Budgeted overhead absorption rate	62.00 per hour	18.00 per hour

Workings:

Metal bashing overhead absorption rate = £814,990/13,145 = £62.00

Metal extrusion overhead absorption rate = £445,500/24,750 = £18.00

Now suppose for Quarter 2 that the overhead absorption rate for the Metal extrusion profit centre had been based on direct machine hours, and was £55 per hour. The actual overheads were £462,500 and the actual machine hours were 8,500 hours.

(b)

	Overheads incurred £	Overheads absorbed £	Difference absorbed £	Under/over absorption
Metal extrusion profit centre	462,500	467,500	5,000	Over

Overheads absorbed = £55 × 8,500 machine hours = £467,500

(c) In Quarter 1 overheads for the Metal bashing profit centre were

over-absorbed	by	£	12,267

Metal bashing overheads absorbed = £62.00 × 12,936 machine hrs = £802,032

Over-absorption = £802,032 – £789,765 = £12,267

....

Task 6

(a)

£	3.60

£223,200/62,000 = £3.60 per unit

(b)

£	3.30

$$\frac{223,200 - 18,600}{62,000} = £3.30$$

(c)

£	2.80

$$\frac{77,500 + 83,700 + 12,400}{62,000} = £2.80$$

(d)

£	173,600

£2.80 × 62,000 = £173,600

(e)

£	204,600

£223,200 – 18,600 = £204,600 (or £3.30 × 62,000 = £204,600)

(f)

	✓
Production cost	
Variable cost	
Overhead cost	
Prime cost	✓

Production cost is the total of the manufacturing costs.

Variable cost are costs which vary directly in line with changes in the level of activity. They can be direct or indirect.

Overhead cost is the sum of the indirect costs.

(g)

	✓
Objectivity	
Integrity	✓
Confidentiality	
Competence	

Objectivity means not allowing bias, conflict of interest or undue influence of others to override judgements.

Confidentiality means not disclosing information to third parties without authority.

Competence means keeping up to date with professional knowledge and skill.

(h)

	✓
Segmented report	✓
Financial report	
Overhead report	
Inventory report	

A financial report may not show details for particular sections of the business.

An overhead report will only show overhead details.

An inventory report will only show inventory details.

(i)

	✓
The department's variable costs only	
The department's total (variable and fixed) costs only	
The department's total costs and revenues	
The department's total costs, revenues, assets and liabilities	✓

A cost centre manager controls costs only.

A profit centre manager controls costs and revenues only.

An investment centre manager controls costs, revenues and investments.

●●●

Task 7

(a)

Term	Description
Limiting factor	Circumstance hindering quantity of units a business may make or sell
Breakeven point	Sales volume where there is neither profit nor loss
Target profit	(Contribution per unit × target activity level) less fixed costs

(b)

> 5,750 units

£46,000/£8 = 5,750

(c)

£	115,000

5,750 × £20 = £115,000

(d)

> 250 units

6,000 – 5,750 = 250 units

(e)

| 8,250 units |

($£20,000/8$) + 5,750 = 8,250

Task 8

	Fixed cost	Variable cost	Semi-variable cost	Stepped cost
Material cost of £3 per unit		✓		
Rent cost of £300	✓			
Labour cost of £10 per unit		✓		
Telephone bill of £20 per quarter plus £0.50 per phone call			✓	
Supervisor cost of £5,000	✓			
Insurance cost of £150	✓			
Machine leasing cost £500 per 4,000 units				✓
Machinery depreciation of £100 based on machine hours used		✓		

Task 9

(a)

	Original budget	Flexed budget	Actual	Variance
Volume sold	250,000	360,000	360,000	
	£000	£000	£000	£000
Sales revenue	5,000	7,200	9,000	1,800
Less costs:				
Direct materials	875	1,260	1,325	–65
Direct labour	1,000	1,440	1,200	240
Fixed overheads	2,450	2,450	3,070	–620
Profit from operations	675	2,050	3,405	

(b)

	✓
Sales revenue	✓
Direct materials	
Direct labour	
Overheads	

(c)

	✓
A decrease in material prices	
An increase in employees' pay	
An increase in material prices	
More efficient usage of direct labour	✓

Task 10

(a)

Appraisal method	Feature
Payback	Ignores the time value of money
NPV	Accept project if appraisal method gives a positive figure
IRR	Discount rate that gives a NPV of zero
NPV	Most important investment criterion

Options:

Payback

IRR

(b) The payback period is **2** years and **4** months

(2,250 – 750 – 1,025) = 475

2 full years taken

475/1,525 = 0.31

0.31 × 12 = 3.72 (4 months)

BPP PRACTICE ASSESSMENT 2
MANAGEMENT ACCOUNTING: COSTING

Time allowed: 2 hours and 30 minutes

Management Accounting: Costing (MMAC)
BPP practice assessment 2

Task 1

(a) Choose the correct words to complete the paragraph.

If costs are increasing, FIFO/LIFO will give a higher profit than FIFO/LIFO as issues, which form cost of sales, are at the earlier, lower/higher prices.

The weighted average method gives a higher profit than LIFO and FIFO/gives a lower profit than FIFO and LIFO/falls somewhere in between the profits given by FIFO and LIFO.

In the long-term, over the life of the business, any such differences will disappear/give the business an advantage/give the business a disadvantage

(b)

The following data relate to inventory item HMF2.

Average usage   200 units per day

Lead time   16–20 days

Reorder level   5,700

What is the approximate number of HMF2 parts carried as buffer inventory?

| | units

(c) Which of the following is the correct formula for the economic order quantity?

☐ $EOQ = \sqrt{\dfrac{2cd}{h}}$

☐ $EOQ = \sqrt{\dfrac{2hd}{c}}$

☐ $EOQ = \dfrac{\sqrt{2ch}}{d}$

☐ $EOQ = \dfrac{\sqrt{2c}}{hd}$

Where   h is the cost of holding one unit in inventory for one year

d is the annual demand

c is the cost of placing an order

Task 2

The material stores control account for a company for March looks like this:

Material stores control account

	£		£
Balance b/d	30,000	Work in progress	100,000
Suppliers	122,500	Overhead control	30,000
Work in progress	45,000	Balance c/d	67,500
	197,500		197,500
Balance b/d	67,500		

Which of the following statements are correct?

(i)   Issues of direct materials during March were £45,000

(ii)   Issues of direct materials during March were £100,000

(iii)   Issues of indirect materials during March were £30,000

(iv)   Purchases of materials during March were £122,500

	✓
(i) and (iv) only	
(ii) and (iv) only	
(ii), (iii) and (iv) only	
All of them	

Task 3

(a) **Complete the columns headed Direct wages and Indirect wages.**

(Note. Zero figures should be entered in cells where appropriate.)

		Direct wages £	Indirect wages £
Basic 35 hours per week at £10 per hour			
Overtime of 4 hours due to machine breakdown			
	Basic 4 hrs @ £10		
	Premium 4 hrs @ £5		
Overtime of 2 hrs at the request of customer			
	Basic 2 hrs @ £10		
	Premium 2 hrs @ £5		
Total			

(b) An employee is paid on a differential piecework system on the following basis.

Up to 750 units produced a week   £2.50 per unit

Units over 750 and up to 1,000   £2.88 per unit

Any units over 1,000   £3.35 per unit

In the week ending 29 June the employee produced 1,075 units.

What is his total gross pay for the week?

£

Task 4

A manufacturing organisation has two production departments, A and B, and two service cost centres, stores and the canteen.

The budgeted overheads for the next period are as follows:

	Total £	A £	B £	Stores £	Canteen £
Indirect wages	75,700	7,800	4,700	21,200	42,000
Rent	24,000				
Buildings insurance	2,000				
Power	6,400				
Heat and light	4,000				
Supervisor's wages – Dept A	10,000				
Machinery depreciation	3,200				
Machinery insurance	2,200				
Total					
Canteen					(49,730)
Stores					

You are also provided with the following information:

	Total	A	B	Stores	Canteen
Net book value of machinery	£300,000	£140,000	£120,000	£15,000	£25,000
Power usage (%)	100%	45%	30%	5%	20%
Number of employees	126	70	40	10	6

	Total	A	B	Stores	Canteen
Supervisor's hours	40	25	15		
Floor area (sq m)	30,000	12,000	8,000	4,000	6,000
Materials requisitions	500	300	200		

The stores staff use the canteen but the canteen makes no use of the stores services.

You are required to:

(a) **Allocate or apportion the overheads to each of the production and service cost centres on a fair basis. (Work to the nearest whole £.)**

(b) **Reapportion the service cost centre costs to the production cost centres using the step down method. (Work to the nearest whole £.)**

Task 5

(a) Budgeted machine hours 17,000

Actual machine hours   21,250

Budgeted overheads   £85,000

Actual overheads   £110,500

Based on the data above:

The machine hour absorption rate is £ _____ per hour.

The overhead for the period was _____ ▼ absorbed by £ _____ .

Picklist:

over-
under-

(b) The accounting entries at the end of a period for production overhead under-absorbed would be **(tick the correct boxes)**:

	Debit	Credit	No entry in this a/c
Overhead control account			
Work in progress account			
Statement of profit or loss			

(c) The overhead absorption rate for product M is £8 per machine hour. Each unit of M requires 1 machine hour. Inventories of product M last period were:

	Units
Opening inventory	6,000
Closing inventory	6,750

The absorption costing profit for the period for product M will be:

☐ higher

☐ lower

than the marginal costing profit. The difference between the two profit figures will be

£	

Task 6

JEB Ltd is planning to produce a new type of chocolate bar called the Jasper bar. It will be manufactured in batches of 80,000 bars.

The following cost estimates have been produced per batch of Jasper bars.

Jasper bar cost estimates	£
Direct material per batch	2,575
Direct labour per batch	2,625
Variable production overheads per batch	2,100
Fixed production overheads per batch	850
Administration, selling and distribution costs per batch	1,025
Total costs	9,175

(a) Calculate the estimated prime cost per BATCH of Jasper bars.

£ [ ]

(b) Calculate the estimated marginal production cost per BATCH of Jasper bars.

£ [ ]

(c) Calculate the estimated full absorption cost of one BATCH of Jasper bars.

£ [ ]

(d) Calculate the estimated marginal production cost of one Jasper bar (round to TWO decimal places).

£ [ ]

(e) Calculate the estimated full absorption cost of one Jasper bar (round to TWO decimal places).

£ [ ]

(f)   Which of the following describes all variable costs?

	✓
Marginal costs	
Period costs	
Prime costs	
Product costs	

(g)   Which of these is an example of unethical behaviour by one of JEB's accounting technicians?

	✓
Calculating tax liabilities without the professional knowledge required	
Being straightforward and honest in business and professional relationships	
Treating JEB's costs as confidential	
Allocating JEB's costs between products objectively	

JEB Ltd's manufacturing department is a cost centre.

(h)   Which of the following does its management control?

	✓
The department's variable costs	
To department's total (variable and fixed) costs	
The department's total costs and revenues	
The department's total costs, revenues, assets and liabilities	

Task 7

ABC Co, is a company producing and selling two types of toys: the elephant and the giraffe. The expected monthly costs and sales information for each toy is as follows.

Toy	Elephant	Giraffe
Sales and production quantity	1,250	1,750
Labour hours per month	120	100
Total sales revenue	£2,500	£3,500
Total direct materials	£200	£350
Total direct labour	£750	£875
Total variable overheads	£50	£140

The total expected monthly fixed costs relating to the production of all toys is £750.

(a) **You are required to complete the table below to show the profit volume ratio for each toy.**

Toy	Elephant £	Giraffe £
Selling price per toy		
Less: Unit variable costs		
Direct materials		
Direct labour		
Variable overheads		
Contribution per toy		
Profit volume ratio (%)		

(b) ABC has decided stop making elephant toys. The expected monthly fixed costs remain at £750. Calculate the breakeven point to the nearest whole unit.

	units

(c) Calculate the margin of safety.

	units

....

Task 8

(a) JLS Ltd operates a job costing system. The company calculates the cost of the job and then adds 20% profit onto the cost to produce a sales price.

The estimated costs for job EIL are as follows.

Direct materials   3 kg @ £5 per kg

Direct labour   4 hours @ £9 per hour

Production overheads are budgeted to be £240,000 for the period and are absorbed on the basis of a total of 30,000 labour hours.

Fill in the table below to calculate the selling price for the job.

Job EIL	£
Direct materials	
Direct labour	
Production overheads	
Total cost	
20% profit	
Selling price for the job	

(b) ABC Ltd uses process costing for some of its products.

Identify the correct journal entries for an abnormal loss:

	Debit	Credit
Process account		
Abnormal loss account		

Task 9

Jumbo Ltd has the following original budget and actual performance for the year ending 31 May:

	Budget	Actual
Volume sold	300,000	410,000
	£000	£000
Sales revenue	9,000	14,350
Less costs:		
Direct materials	1,650	2,460
Direct labour	1,350	1,640
Overheads	3,250	4,010
Operating profit	2,750	6,240

Both direct materials and direct labour are variable costs, but the overheads are fixed.

Complete the table below to show a flexed budget and the resulting variances against this budget for the year. Show the actual variance amount for sales, each cost, and operating profit, in the column headed 'Variance' and indicate whether this is Favourable or Adverse by entering F or A in the final column. If the variance is neither F nor A, enter 0.

	Flexed Budget	Actual	Variance	Favourable F or Adverse A
Volume sold		410,000		
	£000	£000	£000	
Sales revenue		14,350		
Less costs:				
Direct materials		2,460		
Direct labour		1,640		
Overheads		4,010		
Operating profit		6,240		

Task 10

(a) Choose the correct word from the pick list.

The internal rate of return (IRR) is the discount rate that will result in a ⬇ net present value.

Picklist:

negative
positive
zero

If the IRR of a project is [▼] than the organisation's cost of capital then the project should be accepted.

Picklist:

higher
lower

IRR [▼] take into account the time value of money.

Picklist:

does
does not

(b) A project has the following budgeted costs and inflows.

Initial cost	(£350,000)
Inflow 1 year later	£150,000
Inflow 2 years' later	£75,000
Inflow 3 years' later	£95,000
Inflow 4 years' later	£90,000

Calculate the payback period of the proposed project to the nearest whole month.

The payback period is [   ] year(s) and [   ] month(s).

(c) A project has achieved a net present value of £6,000. What does this indicate?

	✔
The project should be rejected	
The project should be accepted	
The project will make £6,000 profit	
The project will generate £6,000 in cash over its life	

BPP PRACTICE ASSESSMENT 2 MANAGEMENT ACCOUNTING: COSTING

ANSWERS

Management Accounting: Costing (MMAC)
BPP practice assessment 2

Task 1

(a) If costs are increasing, FIFO will give a higher profit than LIFO as issues, which form cost of sales, are at the earlier, lower prices.

The weighted average method falls somewhere in between the profits given by FIFO and LIFO.

In the long-term, over the life of the business, any such differences will disappear

(b) 2,100

Buffer inventory   = reorder level – (average usage × average lead time)

                           = 5,700 – (200 × 18)

                           = 2,100

(c) $EOQ = \sqrt{\dfrac{2cd}{h}}$

Task 2

(ii), (iii) and (iv) only

Statement (i) is not correct. A debit to materials with a corresponding credit to work in progress (WIP) indicates that direct materials returned from production were £45,000.

Statement (ii) is correct. Direct costs of production are 'collected' in the WIP account.

Statement (iii) is correct. Indirect costs of production or overhead are 'collected' in the overhead control account.

Statement (iv) is correct. The purchases of materials on credit are credited to the payables account and debited to the materials control account.

Task 3

(a)

		Direct wages £	Indirect wages £
Basic 35 hours per week at £10 per hour		350	
Overtime of 4 hours due to machine breakdown			
	Basic 4 hrs @ £10	40	
	Premium 4 hrs @ £5		20
Overtime of 2 hrs at the request of customer			
	Basic 2 hrs @ £10	20	
	Premium 2 hrs @ £5	10	
Total		420	20

(b)

	£
750 units @ £2.50	1,875
250 units @ £2.88	720
75 units @ £3.35	251.25
	2,846.25

Task 4

(a) and (b)

	Total £	A £	B £	Stores £	Canteen £
Indirect wages	75,700	7,800	4,700	21,200	42,000
Rent	24,000	9,600	6,400	3,200	4,800
Buildings insurance	2,000	800	533	267	400
Power	6,400	2,880	1,920	320	1,280
Heat and light	4,000	1,600	1,067	533	800
Supervisor's wages	10,000	10,000	–	–	–
Machinery depreciation	3,200	1,493	1,280	160	267
Machinery insurance	2,200	1,027	880	110	183
Total	127,500	35,200	16,780	25,790	49,730
Canteen		29,009	16,577	4,144	(49,730)
				29,934	
Stores		17,960	11,974	(29,934)	
		82,169	45,331	–	–

Workings:

Rent, buildings insurance and heat and light are apportioned on the basis of floor area – 12:8:4:6.

Power is apportioned using the percentages given.

Supervisor's wages are allocated directly to department A.

Machinery depreciation and insurance are apportioned on the basis of the net book value of the machinery – 140:120:15:25.

Canteen costs are apportioned according to the number of staff that use it – 70:40:10.

The stores costs are apportioned on the basis of the number of materials requisitions.

••

Task 5

(a) The machine hour absorption rate is £ [5] per hour.

Overhead absorption rate $= \dfrac{\text{Budgeted overheads}}{\text{Budgeted machine hours}}$

$= \dfrac{£85,000}{17,000}$

$= £5$

The overhead for the period was [under] absorbed by [£ | 4,250].

Overhead over-/(under)-absorbed = Overhead absorbed − Overhead incurred

$= (21,250 \times £5) - £110,500$

$= £(4,250)$

(b)

	Debit £	Credit £	No entry in this a/c £
Overhead control account		✓	
Work in progress account			✓
Statement of profit or loss	✓		

Under-absorbed overhead means that the overhead charged to production was too low and so there must be a debit to the statement of profit or loss.

(c) The absorption costing profit for the period for product M will be:

[✓] higher

than the marginal costing profit. The difference between the two profit figures will be

[£ | 6,000]

Difference in profit = change in inventory level × fixed overhead per unit

= (6,000 – 6,750) × (£8 × 1)

= £6,000

The absorption costing profit will be higher because inventories have increased, and fixed overheads have been carried forward in inventory.

Task 6

(a)

£	5,200

(b)

£	7,300

(c)

£	8,150

(d)

£	0.09

(e)

£	0.10

(f)

	✓
Marginal costs	✓
Period costs	
Prime costs	
Product costs	

(g)

	✓
Calculating tax liabilities without the professional knowledge required	✓
Being straightforward and honest in business and professional relationships	
Treating JEB's costs as confidential	
Allocating JEB's costs between products objectively	

JEB Ltd's manufacturing department is a cost centre.

(h)

	✓
The department's variable costs	
To department's total (variable and fixed) costs	✓
The department's total costs and revenues	
The department's total costs, revenues, assets and liabilities	

Task 7

(a)

Toy	Elephant £	Giraffe £
Selling price per toy (W1)	2.00	2.00
Less: Unit variable costs		
Direct materials (W2)	0.16	0.20
Direct labour (W3)	0.60	0.50
Variable overheads (W4)	0.04	0.08
Contribution per toy*	1.20	1.22
Profit volume ratio (%)**	60%	61%

* Contribution = Selling price – Variable costs
** Profit volume ratio = Contribution ÷ selling price × 100%

Workings:

1   Selling price per bottle

Selling price per toy $= \dfrac{\text{Total sales revenue}}{\text{Sales (toys)}}$

Elephant $= \dfrac{£2,500}{1,250} = £2$ per toy

Giraffe $= \dfrac{£3,500}{1,750} = £2$ per toy

2   Direct materials per toy

Direct materials per toy $= \dfrac{\text{Total direct material costs}}{\text{Production volume}}$

Elephant $= \dfrac{£200}{1,250} = £0.16$ per toy

Giraffe $= \dfrac{£350}{1,750} = £0.20$ per toy

3   Direct labour cost per toy

Direct labour cost per toy $= \dfrac{\text{Total direct labour costs}}{\text{Production volume}}$

Elephant $= \dfrac{£750}{1,250} = £0.60$ per toy

Giraffe $= \dfrac{£875}{1,750} = £0.50$ per toy

4   Variable overheads per toy

Variable overheads per toy $= \dfrac{\text{Total variable overhead costs}}{\text{Production volume}}$

Elephant $= \dfrac{£50}{1,250} = £0.04$ per toy

Giraffe $= \dfrac{£140}{1,750} = £0.08$ per toy

(b) Breakeven point = Fixed costs/Contribution per unit

= £750/1.22

= 615 units (to the nearest unit)

(c) Margin of safety = Budgeted sales units – breakeven sales units

= 1,750 – 615

= 1,135

....

Task 8

(a)

Job EIL	£
Direct materials (3 kg × £5)	15.00
Direct labour (4 hours × £9)	36.00
Production overheads (4 hours × £8)*	32.00
Total production cost	83.00
20% profit (£83.00 × 0.2)	16.60
Selling price for the job	99.60

$$* \text{ OAR} = \frac{£240,000}{30,000} = £8 \text{ per labour hour}$$

(b)

	Debit	Credit
Process account		✓
Abnormal loss account	✓	

....

Task 9

	Flexed Budget	Actual	Variance	Favourable (F) or Adverse (A)
Volume sold	410,000	410,000		
	£000	£000	£000	
Sales revenue	12,300	14,350	2,050	F
Less costs:				
Direct materials	2,255	2,460	205	A
Direct labour	1,845	1,640	205	F
Overheads	3,250	4,010	760	A
Operating profit	4,950	6,240	1,290	F

Task 10

(a) The internal rate of return (IRR) is the discount rate that will result in a ⎣ zero ⎦ net present value.

If the IRR of a project is ⎣ higher ⎦ than the organisation's cost of capital then the project should be accepted.

IRR ⎣ does ⎦ take into account the time value of money.

(b) The payback period is **3** years and **4** months.

(c) The project should be accepted.

A net present value is the value of all future cash flows of a project discounted at a particular cost of capital. A positive value indicates the project should be accepted.

BPP PRACTICE ASSESSMENT 3 MANAGEMENT ACCOUNTING: COSTING

Time allowed: 2 hours and 30 minutes

Management Accounting: Costing
BPP practice assessment 3

Task 1

Tagus Ltd had the following receipts of inventory in June.

Date purchased	Quantity	Cost per kg	Total cost £
22 June	500	1.250	625
24 June	392	1.305	511.56

400 kg were issued to production on 26 June.

Drag and drop the correct cost into the cost column of the table below to record the issue on 26 June and to record the inventory balance after the issue using:

- FIFO (first in, first out)
- LIFO (last in, first out)

	Cost
FIFO issue	
LIFO issue	
FIFO balance	
LIFO balance	

£1,136.56	£521.56
£615	£636.56
£625	£500

Task 2

Drag and drop the correct entries into the journal below to record the following FOUR accounting transactions:

Receipt of metal widgets into inventory paying by BACS
Issue of metal widgets from inventory to production
Receipt of metal widgets into inventory paying on credit
Return of metal widgets from production to inventory

The drag and drop choices are:

Debit Inventory, Credit Trade payables control
Debit Inventory, Credit Production
Debit Inventory, Credit Bank
Debit Bank, Credit Goods inward
Debit Trade payables control, Credit Goods inward
Debit Production, Credit Inventory

	Drag and drop choice
Transaction 1	
Transaction 2	
Transaction 3	
Transaction 4	

Task 3

Below is a weekly timesheet for one of Avila Ltd's employees, who is paid as follows:

- For a basic shift every day from Monday to Friday, the basic pay is £13 per hour.

- For any overtime in excess of the basic hours, on any day from Monday to Friday – the extra hours are paid at time-and-a-quarter (basic pay plus an overtime premium equal to quarter of basic pay).

- For any hours worked on Saturday or Sunday, the hours are paid at double time (basic pay plus an overtime premium equal to basic pay).

(a) **Complete the gaps in the table below to calculate the labour cost.**

Employee's weekly timesheet for week ending 7 June

	Hours	Total pay £
Basic pay (including basic hours for overtime)	30	
Mon-Fri overtime premium	4	
Sat – Sun overtime premium	9	
Total		

(b) Employees are also entitled to a bonus of 25% of basic hourly rate for every unit of production in excess of the monthly target. The target for last month was 450 units and employee A produced 490 units.

What was employee A's bonus payment for the month?

£ [   ]

(c) At the end of the month there was a total closing work in progress of 4,200 units which were 85% complete with regard to labour.

What are the equivalent units of production with regard to labour of the closing work in progress?

[   ] units

Task 4

Beppo Ltd's budgeted overheads for the next financial year are:

	£	£
Depreciation of plant and equipment		1,005,188
Power for production machinery		893,750
Rent and rates		130,625
Light and heat		28,875
Indirect labour costs:		
Maintenance	126,438	
Stores	45,063	
General Administration	300,125	
Total indirect labour cost		471,626

The following information is also available:

Department	Net book value of plant and equipment	Production machinery power usage (KwH)	Floor space (square metres)	Number of employees
Production centres:				
Wire plaiting	7,000,000	2,681,250		12
Wire extrusion	3,000,000	1,787,500		10
Support cost centres:				
Maintenance			17,500	4
Stores			10,500	2
General Administration			7,000	3
Total	10,000,000	4,468,750	35,000	31

Overheads are allocated or apportioned on the most appropriate basis. The total overheads of the support cost centres are then reapportioned to the two production centres using the direct method.

- 55% of the Maintenance cost centre's time is spent maintaining production machinery in the Wire plaiting production centre, and the remainder in the Wire extrusion production centre.

- The Stores cost centre makes 70% of its issues to the Wire plaiting production centre, and 30% to the Wire extrusion production centre.

- General Administration supports the two production centres equally.

- There is no reciprocal servicing between the three support cost centres.

Complete the table showing the apportionment and reapportionment of overheads to the two production centres:

	Basis of apportionment	Wire plaiting £	Wire extrusion £	Maintenance £	Stores £	General Admin £	Totals £
Depreciation of plant and equipment	NBV of plant and equipment						
Power for production machinery	Production machinery power usage (KwH)						
Rent and rates	Floor space						
Light and heat	Floor space						
Indirect labour	Allocated						
Totals							

	Basis of apportionment	Wire plaiting £	Wire extrusion £	Maintenance £	Stores £	General Admin £	Totals £
Reapportion Maintenance							
Reapportion Stores							
Reapportion General Admin							
Total overheads to production centres							

Task 5

Next quarter Tagus Ltd's budgeted overheads and activity levels are:

	Glass moulding	Glass extrusion
Budgeted overheads (£)	280,650	300,115
Budgeted direct labour hours	15,550	18,450
Budgeted machine hours	4,350	6,745

(a) **What would be the budgeted overhead absorption rate for each department, if this were set based on their both being heavily automated?**

	✓
Glass moulding £65/hour, Glass extrusion £16/hour	
Glass moulding £18/hour, Glass extrusion £44/hour	
Glass moulding £65/hour, Glass extrusion £44/hour	
Glass moulding £18/hour, Glass extrusion £16/hour	

(b) **What would be the budgeted overhead absorption rate for each department, if this were set based on their both being labour intensive?**

	✓
Glass moulding £65/hour, Glass extrusion £16/hour	
Glass moulding £18/hour, Glass extrusion £44/hour	
Glass moulding £65/hour, Glass extrusion £44/hour	
Glass moulding £18/hour, Glass extrusion £16/hour	

Additional data

At the end of the quarter actual overheads incurred were found to be:

	Glass moulding	Glass extrusion
Actual overheads (£)	315,906	285,550

(c) **Assuming that exactly the same amount of overheads was absorbed as budgeted, what were the budgeted under- or over-absorptions in the quarter?**

	✓
Glass moulding over-absorbed £35,256, Glass extrusion over-absorbed £14,565	
Glass moulding over-absorbed £35,256, Glass extrusion under-absorbed £14,565	
Glass moulding under-absorbed £35,256, Glass extrusion under-absorbed £14,565	
Glass moulding under-absorbed £35,256, Glass extrusion over-absorbed £14,565	

Task 6

Lisboa Ltd has prepared a forecast for the next quarter for one of its small plastic components, ZEST. This component is produced in batches and the forecast is based on selling and producing 2,400 batches.

One of the customers of Lisboa Ltd has indicated that it may be significantly increasing its order level for component ZEST for the next quarter and it appears that activity levels of 3,500 batches and 4,000 batches are feasible.

The semi-variable costs should be calculated using the high-low method. If 6,000 batches are sold the total semi-variable cost will be £14,754, and there is a constant unit variable cost up to this volume.

Complete the table below and calculate the estimated profit per batch of ZEST at the different activity levels: (Work to the nearest whole number until the profit per batch.)

Batches produced and sold	2,400 £	3,500 £	4,000 £
Sales revenue	45,500		
Variable costs:			
Direct materials	11,250		
Direct labour	10,850		
Overheads	6,825		
Semi-variable costs:	8,400		
Variable element			
Fixed element			
Total cost	37,325		
Total profit	8,175		
Profit per batch (to 2 decimal places)	3.41		

Task 7

Product TEST has a selling price of £32 per unit with a total variable cost of £24 per unit. Avignon Ltd estimates that the fixed costs per quarter associated with this product are £43,000.

(a) **Calculate the budgeted breakeven, in units, for product TEST.**

	units

(b) **Calculate the budgeted breakeven, in £s, for product TEST.**

£ [ ]

(c) **Complete the table below to show the budgeted margin of safety in units and the margin of safety percentage if Avignon Ltd sells 5,500 units or 7,000 units of product TEST:**

Units of TEST sold	5,500	7,000
	£	£
Margin of safety (units)		
Margin of safety percentage (nearest whole percentage)		

(d) **If Avignon Ltd wishes to make a profit of £35,000, how many units of TEST must it sell?**

units

(e) **If Avignon Ltd decreases the selling price of TEST by 10p what will be the impact on the breakeven point and the margin of safety, assuming no change in the number of units sold?**

	✓
The breakeven point will decrease and the margin of safety will increase.	
The breakeven point will stay the same but the margin of safety will decrease.	
The breakeven point will increase and the margin of safety will decrease.	
The breakeven point will increase and the margin of safety stay the same.	

Task 8

Batches produced and sold	2,400 £	3,500 £	4,000 £	Cost behaviour
Cost A	12,000	17,500	20,000	
Cost B	14,600	19,000	21,000	
Cost C	15,430	15,430	15,430	
Cost D	21,600	31,500	36,000	

Drag and drop the correct option into the box above to show the correct description for the type of cost. Some costs may be used more than once.

Picklist:

Fixed cost
Semi-variable cost
Stepped cost
Variable cost

....

Task 9

Bilbao Ltd has the following original budget and actual performance for product SCOOT for the year ending 30 June:

	Budget	Actual
Volume sold	50,000	44,000
	£000	£000
Sales revenue	1,750	1,496
Less costs:		
Direct materials	150	130
Direct labour	200	280
Overheads	950	928
Operating profit	450	158

Both direct materials and direct labour are variable costs, but the overheads are fixed.

Complete the table below to show a flexed budget and the resulting variances against this budget for the year. Show the actual variance amount for sales, each cost, and operating profit, in the column headed 'Variance' and indicate whether this is Favourable or Adverse by entering F or A in the final column. If neither F nor A enter 0.

	Flexed Budget	Actual	Variance	Favourable F or Adverse A
Volume sold		44,000		
	£000	£000	£000	
Sales revenue		1,496		
Less costs:				
Direct materials		130		
Direct labour		280		
Overheads		928		
Operating profit		158		

Task 10

One of the moulding machines in the Glass extrusion department is nearing the end of its useful life and Bilbao Ltd is considering purchasing a replacement machine.

Estimates have been made for the initial capital cost, sales income and operating costs of the replacement machine, which is expected to have a useful life of three years:

	Year 0 £000	Year 1 £000	Year 2 £000	Year 3 £000
Capital expenditure	900			
Other cash flows:				
Sales income		540	660	780
Operating costs		300	310	320

The company appraises capital investment projects using a 12% cost of capital.

(a) **Complete the table below and calculate the net present value of the proposed replacement machine (to the nearest £'000):**

	Year 0 £000	Year 1 £000	Year 2 £000	Year 3 £000
Capital expenditure				
Sales income				
Operating costs				
Net cash flows				
PV factors	1.0000	0.8929	0.7972	0.7118
Discounted cash flows				
Net present value				

The net present value is [_____ ▼] .

Picklist:

positive
negative

(b) Calculate the payback period of the proposed replacement machine to the nearest whole month.

The payback period is [_____] year(s) and [_____] month(s).

BPP PRACTICE ASSESSMENT 3
MANAGEMENT ACCOUNTING: COSTING

ANSWERS

Management Accounting: Costing (MMAC)
BPP practice assessment 3

Task 1

	Cost
FIFO issue	£500.00
LIFO issue	£521.56
FIFO balance	£636.56
LIFO balance	£615.00

Workings:

FIFO issue = 400 kg × £1.250 = £500

LIFO issue = (392 kg × £1.305) + (8 kg × £1.250) = £521.56

FIFO balance = (100 kg × £1.250) + (392 kg × £1.305) = £636.56

LIFO balance = (492 kg × £1.250) = £615.00

Task 2

	Drag and drop choice
Transaction 1	Debit Inventory, Credit Bank
Transaction 2	Debit Production, Credit Inventory
Transaction 3	Debit Inventory, Credit Trade payables' control
Transaction 4	Debit Inventory, Credit Production

Task 3

(a) **Employee's weekly timesheet for week ending 7 July**

	Hours	Total pay £
Basic pay (including basic hours for overtime)	30	390
Mon–Fri overtime premium	4	13
Sat–Sun overtime premium	9	117
Total		520

(b) | £ | 130 |

£13 × 25% = £3.25 per unit

40 extra units × £3.25 = £130

(c) | 3,570 | units

4,200 units × 85% = 3,570 units

Task 4

	Basis of apportionment	Wire plaiting £	Wire extrusion £	Maintenance £	Stores £	General Admin £	Totals £
Depreciation of plant and equipment	NBV of plant and equipment	703,632	301,556				1,005,188
Power for production machinery	Production machinery power usage (KwH)	536,250	357,500				893,750
Rent and rates	Floor space			65,312	39,188	26,125	130,625
Light and heat	Floor space			14,438	8,662	5,775	28,875
Indirect labour	Allocated			126,438	45,063	300,125	471,626
Totals		1,239,882	659,056	206,188	92,913	332,025	2,530,064
Reapportion Maintenance		113,403	92,785	(206,188)			
Reapportion Stores		65,039	27,874		(92,913)		
Reapportion General Admin		166,012	166,013			(332,025)	
Total overheads to production centres		1,584,336	945,728				2,530,064

Task 5

(a) The correct answer is Glass moulding £65/hour, Glass extrusion £44/hour

(b) The correct answer is Glass moulding £18/hour, Glass extrusion £16/hour

(c) The correct answer is Glass moulding under-absorbed £35,256, Glass extrusion over-absorbed £14,565

Task 6

Batches produced and sold	2,400	3,500	4,000
	£	£	£
Sales revenue	45,500	66,354	75,833
Variable costs:			
Direct materials	11,250	16,406	18,750
Direct labour	10,850	15,823	18,083
Overheads	6,825	9,953	11,375
Semi-variable costs:	8,400		
Variable element		6,178	7,060
Fixed element		4,164	4,164
Total cost	37,325	52,524	59,432
Total profit	8,175	13,830	16,401
Profit per batch (to 2 decimal places)	3.41	3.95	4.10

Task 7

(a) 5,375 units

(b) £ | 172,000

(c)

Units of TEST sold	5,500 £	7,000 £
Margin of safety (units)	125	1,625
Margin of safety percentage	2%	23%

(d) 9,750 units

(e) The correct answer is: The breakeven point will increase and the margin of safety will decrease.

Task 8

Batches produced and sold	2,400 £	3,500 £	4,000 £	Cost behaviour
Cost A	12,000	17,500	20,000	Variable cost
Cost B	14,600	19,000	21,000	Semi-variable cost
Cost C	15,430	15,430	15,430	Fixed cost
Cost D	21,600	31,500	36,000	Variable cost

Workings:

Cost A

£12,000/2,400 = £5   £17,500/3,500 = £5   £20,000/4,000 = £5

Therefore cost A is a variable cost.

Cost B

Using the high low method:

Variable element = (21,000 – 14,600)/(4,000 – 2,400) = £4

Fixed element = £14,600 – (£4 × 2,400) = £5,000

Check this works for 3,500 units: (3,500 × £4) + £5,000 = £19,000

Therefore cost B is a semi-variable cost.

Cost C is the same at all levels of activity and is therefore a fixed cost.

Cost D

£21,600/2,400 = £9   £31,500/3,500 = £9   £36,000/4,000 = £9

Therefore cost D is a variable cost.

Task 9

	Flexed Budget	Actual	Variance	Favourable F or Adverse A
Volume sold	44,000	44,000		
	£000	£000	£000	
Sales revenue	1,540	1,496	44	A
Less costs:				
Direct materials	132	130	2	F
Direct labour	176	280	104	A
Overheads	950	928	22	F
Operating profit	282	158	124	A

Task 10

(a)

	Year 0 £000	Year 1 £000	Year 2 £000	Year 3 £000
Capital expenditure	(900)			
Sales income		540	660	780
Operating costs		(300)	(310)	(320)
Net cash flows	(900)	240	350	460
PV factors	1.0000	0.8929	0.7972	0.7118
Discounted cash flows	(900)	214	279	327
Net present value	(80)			

The net present value is **negative**.

(b) The payback period is **2** years and **8** months.